Breath | Voice | Fire

Breath | Voice | Fire

Sharon Kimberly Williams

CASCADE Books • Eugene, Oregon

BREATH | VOICE | FIRE

Copyright © 2025 Sharon Kimberly Williams. All rights reserved. Except for brief quotations in critical publications or reviews, no part of this book may be reproduced in any manner without prior written permission from the publisher. Write: Permissions, Wipf and Stock Publishers, 199 W. 8th Ave., Suite 3, Eugene, OR 97401.

Cascade Books
An Imprint of Wipf and Stock Publishers
199 W. 8th Ave., Suite 3
Eugene, OR 97401

www.wipfandstock.com

PAPERBACK ISBN: 979-8-3852-0924-8
HARDCOVER ISBN: 979-8-3852-0925-5
EBOOK ISBN: 979-8-3852-0926-2

Cataloguing-in-Publication data:

Names: Williams, Sharon Kimberly, author.

Title: Breath | voice | fire / Sharon Kimberly Williams.

Description: Eugene, OR: Cascade Books, 2025 | Includes bibliographical references.

Identifiers: ISBN 979-8-3852-0924-8 (paperback) | ISBN 979-8-3852-0925-5 (hardcover) | ISBN 979-8-3852-0926-2 (ebook)

Subjects: LCSH: Racism—United States. | United States—race relations. | Poetry—United States—21st century.

Classification: E185.615 W55 2025 (paperback) | E185.615 (ebook)

VERSION NUMBER 11/11/25

Breath | Voice | Fire is dedicated to the ancestors who journeyed with me through the process of becoming a writer. To the enslaved African and indigenous ancestors who first inhabited this land, my parents Larry and Dorothy Williams, and the generation of civil rights leaders and activists who came before me, this work is your breath, your voice, and your fire made manifest in the earth. As my generation struggles to end racism—racism, that elusive ghost no one has seen or can fully articulate, but we all know is there—please know that we need your guidance as the ghosts of racism haunt us still. Lastly, Breath | Voice | Fire is dedicated to George Floyd and all the victims of the viruses of anti-black racism and COVID-19.

Contents

Acknowledgments | ix

Introduction: Afrofuturism: My Dream for Black America | 1

    1. My Dream for Black America Is to Dream
       the Impossible, Which Is to Dream at All | 1
    2. America in Black and White | 3

Chapter One: Breath | 10

    Part I: A Letter to Sons and Daughters | 11
    Part II: Black Breath | 20
    Part III. Catching Our Breath | 24
    Part IV. Black Feminist/Womanist Breath | 35
    Original Poems and Poetics on Breath | 38

Chapter Two: Voice | 50

    Part I: A Letter to America | 51
    Part II. Silence | 65
    Original Poems and Poetics on Voice | 82

Chapter Three: Fire | 93

    Part I: A Love Letter to the Black Community | 93
    Part II: Embodied Fire | 106
    Part III: Backfire | 114
    Original Poems and Poetics on Fire | 119

Chapter Four: Conclusion: Breath | Voice | Fire: Justice Of The Heart | 124

Part I: A Letter to the Ancestor, George Floyd | 124
Part II. Justice Of The Heart | 132

Chapter Five: Epilogue: Never Stop Breathing: Breath | Voice | Fire as Faith in Action | 138

Bibliography | 143

Acknowledgments

I would like to extend a special thank you to the Drew Theological School faculty and the Africana faculty for all you have done to prepare me for a professional teaching career in theological and religious education. It certainly took a village. Special thanks to Dr. Kenneth Ngwa for granting me the opportunity to serve as a doctoral research associate for the Religion and Global Health Forum while completing this doctoral program. I cannot thank you enough for the clinical research trainee post at Brigham and Women's Hospital at Harvard Medical School, which opened the world of global health advocacy to me. To my dissertation advisor at the Caspersen School of Graduate Studies, Dr. Ron Felber, I am eternally grateful to you for your direction and guidance in developing this dissertation into a work I can be proud of. Also, thank you for introducing me to your method of writing nonfiction by engaging literature. Lastly, I want to thank you for introducing me to *The Plague* the semester before the COVID-19 pandemic arrived, as the timeliness of reading about the crisis of pandemics set the groundwork for my writing. Thank you to Dr. Liana Piehler, my first writing and research teacher at Drew Theological School, and my gracious second reader, for your invaluable artistic and organizational input on this work. Thank you to Dr. Arthur Pressley, Dr. Stephen Moore, and Dr. Jesse Mann for reading the early draft chapters of this work. Lastly, thank you to Professor

Acknowledgments

Robert Carnevale at the Caspersen School of Graduate Education for working to develop my poetry over the years.

I cannot thank you all enough for believing in me. Now, the work begins.

Introduction
Afrofuturism: My Dream for Black America

"It is a radical act for Black people to imagine having a future."[1]

—NALO HOPKINSON

1. My Dream for Black America Is to Dream the Impossible, Which Is to Dream at All

WE HAVE HAD SOME dark days as of late. I write *Breath | Voice | Fire* to provide black America with a road map for survival. Black Americans, the group most susceptible to state-sanctioned violence, need to imagine a future in this country that has never been seen before. Duarte Nunes Leão defines the Brazilian concept of *saudade* as "A longing or nostalgia for what once was and may never be again or for something that never was but the idea of which produces a deep grief and desire, a bittersweet memory of what never was."[2] Thus, it is a deep longing for something one wants but may have never known with the acknowledgment one may never have it again. This is what black Americans experience when true liberation and freedom are imagined. What has been

---

1. Holmes, *Crisis Contemplation*, 123.
2. Bridgeman, "Long Way Home," 219.

Breath | Voice | Fire

accomplished in this nation's history to gain freedom and liberation has been achieved with our Breath (Spirit), Voice, and Fire. From this Breath, Voice, and Fire, we are connected to an imagined, liberated future where we are indeed free. It is a future state of conscious reality where we are not only surviving but thriving. With the emergence of science-fiction films like *Black Panther* on the rise, it is evident that Afrofuturism is currently surging in our culture. This film displays affirmational images of Wakandan warriors and touts technological advancements in future realities never seen by this world. And in this work of cinematic art, we learn that there are ways to transcend a painful past. This is my dream for black America: To never be hindered by the stigma of blackness placed upon our people by white supremacy. To transcend racial barriers and unjust boundaries using our breath, voice, and fire.

Afrofuturism may provide a road map. Afrofuturism, a term coined by Mark Dery in 1964, was already established as a genre. Afrofuturism can be understood as follows:

Afrofuturism—broadly speaking—takes black histories and realities and adds a dose of magic, mysticism, superpowers, or all three to create new worlds where the protagonists are black people. These stories can be sci-fi, they can be horror, they can imagine a past that never happened or a distant future that by today's standards seems impossible.[3] The genre of Afrofuturism stretches to the subversive, future-forward aesthetic of artists like Sun Ra, Parliament-Funkadelic, and novelist Octavia E. Butler and her "Patternist" series. For Afrodiasporic artists, the genre provides a fertile landscape to dream up a future outside the limits of white supremacy; it is powerful because it dares to dream a future for Afrodiasporic people.[4]

---

3. Holmes, *Crisis Contemplation*, 123
4. Holmes, *Crisis Contemplation*, 123.

Introduction

2. America in Black and White

What does it mean for black Americans to dream the impossible dream? The struggle is real, not imagined, for black Americans. The conditions we have met in this strange land have forced us to understand our place in it. Institutionalized racism is a problem that can be best understood when one measures racial disparities in black and white. Many think there is no organized effort by white people to harm black people in America. Yet many of the violent socio-economic systems in this country are designed to prosper whites and punish black people. The metrics on racial progress in America make the case that there are significant racial disparities in how our systems serve each ethnic group based on their assigned race.

America in Black and White: How Much Progress Has Been Made?

Our success and survival in this nation must be related to how well we transcend a fixed reality based on an unequal society, a fact that is not subject to change much in the near future. The truth is that things may not change much for a large majority of blacks, due to barriers to entry into the upper echelons of economics in our society. But as we focus on our internal and external breath, voice, and fire, one learns to navigate a violent, hostile world that works systemically to maintain the status quo. This world we inhabit, called America, is a complex world full of agendas and compromise.

This world, America, is one that justice seekers can only transform slowly. The ideology of Afrofuturism for black Americans contains a powerful hope that wins over pessimism and the dark past that haunts our dreams. We can imagine without limits to dream the impossible dream because the longing for what we know our reality can be is intense. Afrofuturistic jazz legend Sun Ra said, "The possible has been tried and failed. Now it is time to try the impossible."[5] It is in the creativity of our breath, voice,

5. Holmes, *Crisis Contemplation*, 8.

and fire that we learn to dream dreams and make the impossible possible. The cosmic consciousness of our breath, voice, and fire transcends this world's harsh sociopolitical and economic realities. It allows us to move to the realm of all potential and possibilities. First and foremost, the goal now and forever will be survival of black people in the future. We must begin now with the help of our ancestors to imagine ourselves in new realities where we are thriving in all areas so that we can transform our communities into the futuristic examples they are intended to be. In doing so, we must never abandon the indigenous knowledge of our ancestors as we shift into the modern, technological realities of the future.

Breath | Voice | Fire: The Spiritual Meets the Political

Through the engagement of the spiritual and the political, black American leaders like Dr. Martin Luther King Jr. have shaped a unique model for the leadership of oppressed people. *Breath | Voice | Fire* expresses this symbiotic relationship between the spiritual and the political. bell hooks engages this notion of the spiritual and the political eloquently as she states,

> I have tried here in this writing to speak of how spiritual inner movement flows outward, the way the fire within burns with an intensity that brings light, vision, and warmth to every aspect of my being. It is this sacred fire that can be felt in my writing. Anyone who has known the sweet communion of the Holy Spirit, the ecstasy of divine love, knows how difficult it is to give such experience to words. These words I have written, a confession of my faith, are necessary testimony. Even though they can never name religious experience fully, I have wanted to locate that meeting place of spirituality and progressive politics in my life.[6]

In *Remembering Rapture*, hooks mentions the influences that have developed her unique "spiritual meets the political" writing

6. hooks, *Remembering Rapture*, 123.

Introduction

style, which are King, Howard Thurman, Thich Nhat Hanh, Henri Nouwen, James Cone, Cornel West, and Malcolm X. For hooks, spiritual practice sustains and nurtures progressive politics and enhances the liberation struggle. I thank God for bell hooks's example of written expression on the spiritual and the political, which serves as a model for this writing. *Breath | Voice | Fire* as an understanding of how the spiritual meets the political is a critical part of my dream for black America: a dream that challenges the morality of the political issues of the day. We cling to peace and social justice activism in this season of rampant anti-black violence. We look to our spiritual leaders who understand the importance of addressing the political matters that plague their communities. Mahalia Jackson stated the case perfectly with the spiritual she sang at the 1963 March on Washington: "How I got over, how I got over. My soul looks back and wonders how I got over!"

I consider *Breath | Voice | Fire* a tool of improvisational transformation and transcendence for community leaders to utilize in addressing the survival of black Americans. It is a literary tool grounded in Afrofuturism as possibilities, if you will, which brings cosmic hope to an oppressed people. *Breath | Voice | Fire* as a work of creative nonfiction is intended to engage our consciousness so we can become change agents and cultural representations of American culture. *Breath | Voice | Fire* prepares us to address the disorder, chaos, and crises we are currently experiencing. We need the gift of our breath, our voice, and our fire to ground us and transcend white supremacy.

Although I use lyrical language to explain the problem of white supremacy, my dream for black America is that we never see ourselves as victims of white supremacy. We will create a perfect union in America through our collective, transformed consciousness. *Breath | Voice | Fire* can be realized as Afrofuturistic imagination that dreams of a better future that achieves impossible dreams by joining a collective consciousness that works outside the margins drawn out by white supremacy.

How do we imagine futures when we still cling to our painful memories of the past? How do we work through our breath, voice, and fire to begin the transformative, internal work of no longer seeing ourselves as victims but as sojourners along with our white brothers and sisters in this American experiment? We must transcend the old vision of who we are and achieve a new understanding of how we see ourselves. We must transform and transcend the old identity and continue to move toward self-determination and self-reliance. We must transform our consciousness and elevate ourselves to function on a higher plane. We must continue the sacred journey of the American experiment, first surviving, then transcending into a place of collective consciousness where most of us are thriving, not struggling. The same performance of blackness as an embodiment of our experience must evolve. We must transcend the existential crisis of the American color line and gather those once distant possibilities within our reach.

Photographer Mikael Owunna stated, "The question I asked myself here was: How can I transfigure black bodies from sites of death and state-sanctioned violence in transcendent forms into vessels of eternal cosmic life?"[7] We can achieve this. As we transform our identity through our breath, voice, and fire, we move our beings from death to eternal life. But first, everything about how we are perceived in society and how we perceive ourselves must change. In black America, we must see ourselves through our interconnectedness to the universe, God, each other, and nature. Through our interconnectedness, we are healed from our past traumas and can transcend reality and realize our cosmic futures.

Today, there is a general lack of outrage over the loss of precious things that will never be returned to us, and it is precisely this lack of outrage that shows us just how sick society is. This lack of outrage connects to the lack of a love of justice we identified through the Black Lives Matter movement. As a nation, we are disconnected. In our disconnectedness, we lose things. Precious things. How exactly are we disconnected?

- We have lost our connection/reverence for God/spirituality, and there is no outrage or responsibility.

---

7. Holmes, *Crisis Contemplation*, 126.

Introduction

- We experience disconnection with nature as we have lost endangered species, and there is no outrage or responsibility.
- We experience disconnection with humanity as we have lost our ability to live compassionately, and there is no outrage or responsibility.

In conclusion, I dream for black America an impossible dream to be made possible: That we may continually strive to protect precious things like black lives. *Breath | Voice | Fire* was created as a response that atones for and heals from the loss of precious things we have lost along the way. As we reclaim our precious breath, voice, and fire through transformation and transcendence, there is renewed hope for the future of black Americans.

Chapter I: Breath: The breath chapter opens with a letter to the daughters and sons of a divided America written by the narrator (the Psalmist). The letter is prefaced by a quote from James Baldwin and the haunting refrain of Frantz Fanon's philosophy of the all-encompassing "White Song" that positions whiteness as a metaphor for the ultimate source of power in the strange land defined as America. The letter follows with a lyrical mosaic entitled "White Noise" to critique American hypocrisy through the symbolism of "Necks"—white noise and what it doesn't hear and lastly, necks as a bridge to and from articulation and strangulation. The letter is followed by poetry and prose that highlights the difficulty for marginalized blacks and women, created in the image of God, to breathe in a divided America.

Chapter II: Voice: The voice chapter opens with a letter to America written by the narrator (the Psalmist) and is prefaced by a lyric from two Negro spirituals, "Nobody Knows the Trouble I've Seen" and "Over My Head, I See Trouble in the Air." This chapter warns about what happens when people are silent and speaks of voice through the lens of silence to provide a foundation for what a community feels. Feelings of suffocation versus inspiration. Pride of "voice" versus the humiliation of a people smothered in silence. It shows silence as the culprit, a co-conspirator with anti-black racism sentiments. "Good people" are urged to break their silence in ways that challenge the American status quo on racial issues. The problem with the pursuit of racial justice is revealed in the example of the myth of Sisyphus, which tells of a character who spent eternity rolling a boulder up a hill just to see it roll back down again.

Chapter III: Fire: The fire chapter opens with a love letter to the black community that likens America to a divided house on fire written by the narrator (the Psalmist). It is prefaced by quotes from Cornel West and Sonia Sanchez, which ask the community, "Where is your fire?" And then by urging the community to find it (or "Catch the Fire") and pass it on before it's too late. The Psalmist suggests the community should fight fire with their spiritual "fire." The letter is followed by two sections of poetry and prose to demonstrate what it means to be on fire for justice. The biblical narrative of the prophet Jeremiah's testament, "Fire shut up in my bones" and the tongues of prophetic fire featured on the day of Pentecost are used as models for fostering mobilization and change. Most profoundly, this chapter grapples with the question, "If tongues could speak, what would they say about you, America? Would they say the game is rigged?"

Chapter IV: Conclusion: Breath | Voice | Fire: Justice of the Heart: The conclusion opens with a letter to the ancestor George Floyd written by the narrator (the Psalmist). The letter pays homage to George and all those who have died due to police violence. The Psalmist challenges those who remain here in America to move toward reconciliation and redemption. This section of the writing is prefaced by a lyrical quote from Stevie Wonder, "Someday there's gotta be a justice of the heart," as a response to George's murderer.

The purpose of this section is to let the ancestor George Floyd know that his life *mattered* and urge him to continue to watch over us as we struggle to make this divided country whole. The letter emphasizes to Floyd all the things we learned from both his life and his death. As the Psalmist takes a journey with the Tin Man

Introduction

from *The Wizard of Oz* to find the heart of the nation, she begs the question: "What is in the heart of this nation: Love or hatred?" She also challenges everyone to examine what is in their hearts on the issue of anti-black violence: hearts of stone or hearts of flesh?

V. *Chapter Five: Epilogue: Never Stop Breathing: Breath | Voice | Fire as Faith in Action:* The epilogue opens with a summary of where we are four years after the death of George Floyd as it urges the reader to *Never Stop Breathing.* It tells the story of how the details of the final moments of George Floyd's life began with a citizen video captured innocently by a young bystander. It also tells the story of the author working as a graduate student and student research associate for the *Religion and Global Health Forum,* and writing a dissertation during peculiarly turbulent times. In the end, the greatest part of the author's education was learning from her professor, Dr. Kenneth Ngwa, "Why We Don't Stop Breathing" and how her call to action, *Breath | Voice | Fire,* would forever shape her worldview. In the spirit of the Black Arts Movement poet Sonia Sanchez, I say, *"Where is your breath?" "Where is your voice?" "Where is your fire?"*

Chapter One

Breath

"How can we sing the Lord's song in a strange land?"

—Psalm 137:4

"All around me the white man, above the sky tears at its navel, the earth rasps under my feet, and there is a white song, a white song. All this whiteness that burns me..."[1]

—Frantz Fanon

"I attest to this. The world is not white. It never was white. Cannot be white. White is a metaphor for power and that is a simple way of describing Chase Manhattan Bank."[2]

—James Baldwin

---

1. Fanon, *Black Skin, White Masks*, 112.
2. Baldwin, *I Am Not Your Negro*, 107.

Breath

Part I: A Letter to Sons and Daughters

1. Introduction: White Song

Beloved, here are a few things you need to know for your journey in this strange land.

America is a strange land. America's song is not "America the Beautiful." America's song is the white song of supremacy. This song has always been a mediocre tune at best. America's *Song of Supremacy* has always been such an absurd selection to play in the "land of the free, the home of the brave." A song of power, it is the soundtrack of our lives that lulls sheep into unrestful, slumbering days. This white song is whiteness beyond white robes that tells the history of a nation deeply wounded by its past. A nation that longs to heal. The white song, the song of supremacy, is a metaphor for power. The antithesis to the American anthem "America the Beautiful," proclaims God's will, "crown thy good with brotherhood," but brotherhood is not offered. The white song is sung as a weapon. It vows never to be defeated.

What is the origin of this white song? The story of America is far from a straightforward tale of heroes and villains. From and before the song of King Cotton white as snow, there is no moral rationale, no explanation for this song's origins. For the white song just is. As the founding fathers began to weave the white song into the cultural fabric of the nation, one can see that its sonic presence was deliberate. Calculated. A song of violent systems, it maintains an imbalance to keep its peculiar version of law and order. This world in the shadows of justice has little room for heroes to make their mark as historical martyrs. This song, a mighty multiplier of wealth for America's sons and daughters, cannot play forever. Will this song change before it is too late?

America is a strange land. There is an awakening in the streets of America that has nothing to do with white against black. This awakening is about black and white singing together a new song of justice that works to dismantle the song of supremacy. Young people chant, "Black Lives Matter, Black Lives Matter" as counterculture's response of resistance to the all-encompassing power of the white song. Those who do not want America to know itself and its hidden legacy and authentic self-identity will challenge the resistance. These proponents of the status quo are content to replay that familiar refrain of the white song into perpetuity. This current awakening is about a breaking, or an interruption, of the song signals a reckoning. Some would maintain that the American governance systems are broken, suggesting they can be fixed. I am here to say that the systems are not broken.

On the contrary, the systems are working exactly as they were intended. This song was designed to play into eternity. A haunting song, sung first by ghosts of America's past, is a hymn of sin that sealed the fate of a young country's future. A superpower with an unreconciled past that present and future generations will never be able to rise above. As Fanon suggests in the opening quote of this chapter, the ancestors of old spoke from the perspective of this being the "white man's world" and that one day, they would need to reconcile either with black folks or with God. Their choice. The white song has always been America's weakness. It is its Achilles' heel. Like kryptonite, the song that appears to give power robs the nation of its true power and moral authority. Thus, the song of supremacy's sound waves pull America under and drown the country. From the deep, we awaken to the song. In due season, just in time to meet what the ancestors have scheduled. A reckoning? Perhaps.

America is a strange land. Just stop dreaming, America! The dream of the white song is the American Dream or a nightmare for some. A secret song that hides in plain sight behind perfect white picket fences and veneers of greatness. The song knows who you are, America. It knows who I am, too. The white song is the American identity. The song distorts American ideals and offers false realities against God's justice, in absurd ways. Like the padded white walls of an insane asylum, we live in an America centered on whiteness expressed through a song that is singing us to madness. But we are not crazy. Straitjackets restrain our minds, safeguarding the white lie. With America's history of chattel slavery and lynching, how dare the white song continue to play into the twenty-first century? What has the song done to us? What will it do? How has it shaped our lives in ways we do not even realize?

A sarcastic song that whispers loudly, "Black Lives Don't Matter," hushes protesters with a deadly silent rule of power. The work of the song has been so effective that it need not even open its mouth to communicate its presence, which is all around. Ever present. All the time. The system is efficient and effective. The song of supremacy feeds on the hate needed to sustain it. The white song teaches America something profound about violence, sickness, and the viruses that attack its body and soul. White song, the anthem that birthed this nation, the song is you, America. It locks your identity in a choke hold, vowing never to let go. The song of supremacy plays continuously in the heart of your nation even when you do not see it. The song is present in every neighborhood, school, and workplace. Song of power, how far are you willing to go?

America is a strange land. The sound of this song reverberates in the hearts of far too many good men and women. Let not this song cause the fall of a great nation. Great not because of this song, but despite it. Those who live the American experience in black bodies know there is no escaping the white song. This song, which our forefathers and foremothers knew well for generations, has reigned supreme for all our days. This hypnotic song that has taken us beyond the parameters of the limitations of our minds.

Quite simply, it is a song written to teach the sons and daughters of enslaved and indigenous people all the written and unwritten rules that establish their place and position within American society. A song that decides which people should live and which people should die is a song designed to make those same sons and daughters of enslaved people want to give up, give in, and admit defeat. They are literally and figuratively imprisoned by the white song, a song designed to break men's souls as they are faced with the difficulty of reconciling their human existence as "a problem." Everyone is blinded by the white song that covers the color and beauty of diversity. Lyrics like lashes on the backs of the righteous. That is what the white song feels like to my people and me.

But there is a reckoning.

Those who sing the white song are assured that the world is theirs. Seduced by the same song that makes villains into heroes, they are the sons and daughters of a lie that works against the justice of God. No one escapes the song, for it is a meticulous timekeeper. We are all the victims of it. Those white sons and daughters also remain prisoners of the song, inheriting the trauma of executing crimes against humanity. As long as the white song continues to play, America will be reminded of the debt it owes.

But know that we all owe a debt. As long as the white song continues to play out in systematic racism that causes an existential threat to black people, no one will be truly free. Reconcile with God or with us, your black brothers and sisters. Only the power of love can dismantle the white song. Until the day the immortal song of justice returns to play its final encore, we will continue to endure knowing that no war waged against the will of God can be won. Justice will prevail and the song will be no more.

2. White Noise

America is a strange land. Between the imago Dei and me are the white song and all its noise. This white noise blocks me from entering the house. This sonic song produces a white noise like an unstable static only audible at high frequencies. The purpose of this noise is to attempt to drown out the voice of God, who is also chanting, "Black Lives Matter." Black bodies were created in the image of God. Therefore, Black Lives Matter. When the white noise captured and enslaved Africans, black lives mattered then. Black lives matter now. When the white noise lynched black bodies from the gentle Southern trees, black lives mattered then. Black lives matter now. When the white noise authorized state-sanctioned police violence and mass incarceration, black lives mattered then. Black lives matter now. When the white noise ignored the health crisis of COVID-19 in our communities, black lives mattered then. Black lives matter now.

Who decides who lives and who dies? Who decides which lives matter in society? The song lyric "Kill dem before they grow,"

Breath

by Bob Marley, summarizes American necropolitics of death inherent in the noise of the white song. The white song has had many significant performances of war in America. Performances of genocide and erasure. A song of subtraction sung by the grim reaper, our ancestors, revealed this then in the spiritual, "There's a man goin' round taking names." Hands up, don't shoot! Can't you hear me through the White Noise? I said I CAN'T BREATHE! "There is still a man going around taking names." George Floyd, Trayvon Martin, Breonna Taylor, and so many others. And the white song plays on and on and on through the white noise. Never missing a beat.

Yes, *America is a strange land, indeed.* The white noise of the song of supremacy creates static so one cannot see or hear clearly. Before you pull the trigger, officer, look closely through the white noise. When you see the person on the other end of your weapon, you should see the image of God. Listen closely through the white noise. In the name of justice, we must expose the hidden song in the hearts of every man or woman. The song of supremacy is "goin' round takin' names." And the song that is killing us must be dismantled. If the black lives matter movement is a revolutionary moment, the victory will be *when they see us* in the image of God. And when they see us in the image of God, the white song will no longer be needed. And nothing will need to be hidden in the white noise as we sing our new song in "our" strange land. Black sons and daughters with white sons and daughters united.

> And O my people, out yonder, hear me, they do not love your neck unnoosed and straight. So, love your neck; put a hand on it, grace it, stroke it, and hold it up. And all your inside parts that they'd just as soon slop for hogs, you got to love them. The dark, dark liver—love it, love it, and the beat and beating heart, love that too. More than eyes or feet. More than lungs that have yet to draw free air. More than your life-holding womb and your life-giving private parts, hear me now love your heart. For this is the prize.[3]
> —Toni Morrison, *Beloved*

3. Morrison, *Beloved*, 105.

Breath | Voice | Fire

3. Necks

America is a strange land. Better mind your necks!

"Mind your neck!" Black children from neighborhoods like mine would say this in the schoolyards and on the playgrounds of our enchanted concrete jungles. I never thought much about how that inconsequential, common phrase started. It probably started in any one of the many urban neighborhoods of New York in the 1970s. We had our inner world of colloquial language that was only ours, and it did not need to be explained to anyone outside our gates. As a child who used that phrase, I did not know then that the neck, so inconsequential and unassuming, says so much about the multifaceted legacy of black people in America.

From the Jim Crow laws of the 1950s and sixties to the New Jim Crow of today, the neck connects us to the ancestral memory of every lynched dream of black persons born in America. The neck is a bridge to the truth of our story in America. A truth that must be told. Life and death are concentrated on the necks of those who walk through America in black bodies. We are never far from falling prey to the paradoxical dilemma of the New Jim Crow that defines the character of the modern American criminal justice system. For us, the neck symbolizes our strangled possibilities of freedom from a system that simply does not love our necks. So, "we better mind our necks!"

In this era of the New Jim Crow, one must not forget that a society is judged by the quantity and quality of its prison system. The American justice system is a mirror that tells us who we are as a nation—reflecting and magnifying every injustice that defines our character as Americans complicit in the behavior. With every public video of police violence, the images are telling the world in the plainest of terms who we are, and that black life does not matter in America. These murdering, mirroring reflections reveal the truth of our American identity and show us who we are as opposed to who we tell ourselves we are, as proclaimed in the Declaration of Independence. "We hold these truths to be self-evident, that all men are created equal, that they are endowed by their Creator with certain unalienable Rights, that among these are Life, Liberty and the pursuit of Happiness."

Perhaps when we used the phrase "Mind your neck!" so casually as children, we urged each other to tend to our own business and stay out of trouble because trouble was so pervasive. Things could take a dangerous turn in an instant. Even though we could not articulate it properly, we knew our world was not safe, so it would be best just to mind and be mindful of the racialized systems that tried to control our world and limit our breath. I never really thought much about how much trouble could come from the white gaze on black necks until now.

One day it became clear that I was no longer a child. Like the biblical verse, "When I was a child, I thought as a child." But when I became an adult, I knew the white gaze was upon me. Monitoring. Controlling. It had always been there, whether I noticed it before or not. This current season of black citizens dying while in the custody of law enforcement has taught me that a lot of our trouble with law enforcement starts with the white gaze on black necks. This gaze imagines how blackness interrupts the rhythm of the white song and spoils the purity of a nation's understanding of the American Dream. It is all there contained in the narrative, the long legacy of the black neck in America. A cautionary tale for sure, but one that has profoundly and prophetically found a way to be told now. In the breath of our ancestral hopes and promises, those messages still speak to us today: *"America is a strange land. Better mind your neck, children! Hear me; they don't love your neck."*

As God is our witness, Lord knows we try to do just that. But for those experiencing this American strange land in black bodies, we are never free from the white gaze and the systemic lynching that manifests on multiple levels in our society. Toni Morrison warned, "Hear me, they don't love your neck unnoosed and straight." The tactics of yesterday's Jim Crow lynching are alive and well today, singing the same white song of supremacy. Today, they still do not love black necks unnoosed and straight. The Equal Justice Initiative recently reported that 6,500 black people had been lynched in America since the Thirteenth Amendment of

1865.[4] This amendment, which renders persons imprisoned to the status of chattel slavery as they are defined as the property of the States, the first reign of terror and lynching by a noose around the neck, represents a tactic of the Old Jim Crow.

The New Jim Crow is where we are today, with black communities being over-policed for minor offenses—and lynched in the prison industrial complex, a capitalist system that feeds on and profits from human capital in the form of black necks. Even when one minds one's neck, black necks are still not safe when there are so many empty prisons that must be filled. Because of the loophole in the Thirteenth Amendment, the state has the right to continue the legacy of slavery and lynching through its criminal justice system that captures black bodies. *"America's a strange land. Better mind your neck, children! Hear me; they don't love your neck."*

So, love your necks, black sons and daughters, and do not ever stick them out too far. That shows off their beauty. In the immortal words of our beloved ancestor, Toni Morrison, you must *love your neck; put a hand on it, grace it, stroke it, and hold it up.* But be ever so mindful. For the white gaze is upon the necks that do not mind their own business—as we challenge the morality of America's business—which is the business of the white song, and as we challenge the criminal justice system that *captures black people by our necks to control our breath.*

The same white song that selfishly covets the spoils for its own had nothing for my ancestors and has less than nothing for me, except for a knee on my neck. It has nothing for our children except for a knee on their neck. As that state-sanctioned knee sits in comfort on our collective necks, singing the white song into eternity, know that it is a legacy that intends to take, exploit, and use, not share. But when the day of reckoning is upon us, there will be no more lynching, *capturing black people by our necks to control our breath.* Until then, remember the lessons so many of us learned as children on the playground in the wisdom of our mystical, whimsical world that was only ours. We better take heed and mind our necks. Trouble is in the air we breathe.

---

4. Ruiz-Grossman, "At Least 2,000 More Black Americans."

Breath

As the lambs for America's sacrifice, mind your black sacred necks, sons and daughters, while you still have breath—while you still have a story to tell. Mind them and love them lest you find the knee of the New Jim Crow upon your neck, resting, slow and steady, with a righteous condemnation that comes with the full, state-sanctioned power of the white song to suffocate your black breath and silence your black voice as it struggles to maintain the breath for a new song in a strange land.

Eternally yours,

The Psalmist

Dreams of a Father as Dreams of Future Breath
By Sharon Kimberly Williams

My father never gave me many gifts,
He was never good at celebrating,
Birthdays or holidays,
Before he passed away,
He gave me his collection of jazz albums,
From scat to bebop to swing,
Concealed within the rhythmic collection of,
Sarah, Miles, and Coltrane,
Hidden was an original live recording of,
The 1963 *March on Washington,*
With the iconic *I Have a Dream* speech.

Growing up, both my parents (especially my father),
Were particularly proud people,
They had marched with Dr. King,
So as much as I appreciated,
Having the prize,
My father's jazz collection,
Having an original recording of the March,
Was like having my very own piece of,
The Movement,
To better understand my father,
What was life for a Black man in those times?

What American Dream?
Where was that dream for him then?

Breath | Voice | Fire

>Where is that dream for so many now?
>Then and now,
>So distant, so out of reach for so many,
>An unfamiliar modality for most,
>Who dares to live life in a different key?
>Who dares to dance to a different rhythm?
>For those who hope against hope,
>For harmony?

Sometimes all a father has to give his children are his dreams.
Sometimes the dream is enough,
For those who hope against hope,
Who only want to dance their dance in the key of life,
When floating through the abyss,
Far from all those who have actualized their American Dream,
The dreams of a father are the gift of hope.

Part II: Black Breath

"My God, why has thou forsaken me?"

—Psalm 22:1

"I can't breathe!"

—George Floyd et al.

I had to leave [America]; I needed to be in a place where I could breathe and not feel someone's hand on my throat."[5]

—James Baldwin

---

5. Coles, "James Baldwin Back Home."

Breath

1. Introduction: The Existential Crisis of the Problem of Blackness in Genesis

When Négritude poets Aimé Césaire and Léopold Sédar Senghor raised this critical, three-part question—"*Who am I? Who are we? What are we in this White world?*"[6]—one could conclude that the narrative of the people of African Diaspora has its genesis in the theodicy of the problem as defined in Psalm 22:1: "My God, why has thou forsaken me?" W. E. B. Du Bois approached this same question of the problem between God and the existence of the descendants of Africa from another perspective when he so eloquently stated in *The Souls of Black Folks*, "The problem of the twentieth century is the problem of the color line." Du Bois challenged the people of the Africa Diaspora to examine their lives when he posited the question, "How does it feel to be a problem?"[7]

Césaire, Senghor, and Du Bois concluded that the mere existence of the people of the African Diaspora presents a problem—much like questions of theodicy—that cannot be easily resolved. Scholar of Africana philosophy Lewis Gordon describes theodicy or "the problem of evil" as God's justice or the justice of God. The question of problem people also raises questions for postcolonialism considerations. From the Greek words *theós* (god) and *díkē* (justice), theodicy means justifying God's goodness in the face of evil or, more simply, the justice of God.[8]

Therefore, race as a specific problem of evil presents an existential concern for the people of the African Diaspora that should be studied within the context of theodicy. The problem of evil in theodicy is much like the problem of evil in race discrimination. What does it imply when one believes being a problem results from being forsaken by God? As Du Bois famously observed, the splitting of worlds and mental consciousness according to the norms of American society and its contradictions is the conflict of twoness

---

6. Diagne, "Négritude."
7. Diagne, "Négritude."
8. Gordon, *Introduction to Africana Philosophy*, 76.

(or double consciousness).⁹ For the people of the African Diaspora for whom this concept of double consciousness exists, the problem of evil is connected to the question of their very existence. Thus it calls into question God's relationship with the African Diaspora. Within this state of double consciousness, how does one breathe? What is the role of breath in affirming one's humanity?

2. Genesis: The Problem of Evil and Being Created in God's Image as a Contradiction

"And God (Elohim) said, Let us make man in our image, after our likeness..."

—GENESIS 1:27

Humanity is created in God's perfect image, including the people of the African Diaspora. In Hebrew, the fact that we were all created *betselem 'Elohim*—or in the image of God—is one of the most important messages to the Africana world.¹⁰ This is the imago Dei's importance in reconciling the African Diaspora's humanity. We must reconcile questions of theodicy and otherness against the knowledge that we were made in the likeness of God. It is so relevant because we are a people who know what it means to be deemed less than human.¹¹ One must use care in using the terminology "image of God" in deciding which groups would be included and which would be excluded. One might ask, "What about the souls of black folks in this context of the imago Dei? Does the biblical concept of the imago Dei present a contradiction for those who wish to uphold systems of racism, sexism, and classism? The imago Dei and the concept of "otherness" regarding the question of race are in complete contradiction. The people of the African Diaspora were created in the image of God, which means they are not a problem in that the work of the creator is perfect. Du Bois

9. Gordon, *Introduction to Africana Philosophy*, 76.
10. Sadler Jr., "Genesis," 71.
11. Sadler Jr., "Genesis," 72.

spent a good portion of his life trying to justify the humanity of the people of the African Diaspora as he continued to pose his question to broader society, "How does it feel to be a problem?"[12]

His work challenged anti-black racism at its core by emphasizing the most polarizing social construct conceived for perpetuating racialized, systematic evil: the "color line." The racialized "other" and the concept of imago Dei directly contradict race in that humans can only be made in God's image. In his questioning, Du Bois challenged the status quo to demonstrate how people were not equal. Because of the African Diaspora's racialized "otherness," Du Bois had to make a case for Africana people's basic humanity. Yet, it is evident in Genesis 1:27, which reads, "And God said, Let us make man in our image, after our likeness." Therefore, it follows that logically, the existence of the ones created by God in the image of God cannot make an existential problem for the rest of society when all humans are part of the same race—the human race.

The imago Dei represents that we are created in the image of a God who suffers along with us. And it is through their suffering that the people of the African Diaspora are most like God, which means being made in the image of God, and racism is a direct contradiction to the principle that all humans are created equally.

"And the LORD *God formed man of the dust of the ground and breathed into his nostrils the breath of life, and man became a living soul."*

—GENESIS 2:7

What is the importance of breath as it relates to the image of God? Again, Du Bois posed the question *How does it feel to be a problem* (when the problem is that some believe you have no soul)? *The Souls of Black Folk* was written partially in response to theologian Charles Carroll's *The Negro: A Beast or in the Image of God*. There Carroll argues that the "Negro" is more beast than a human made in the image of God.[13] Denying that the people of the

---

12. Du Bois, *Souls of Black Folk*, 9.
13. Carroll, *Negro*.

African Diaspora share the breath of the divine with all humanity contradicts Genesis 2:7. Carroll's writing attempts to diminish the humanity of the people of the African Diaspora, laying the groundwork for what is to come and creating the justification for subjugating them among human souls.

Because they are deemed a problem by some justifies the evil and separates the people of the African Diaspora from God. How would a just God allow this to happen to his people? Theodicy says God is justified in the face of evil. This is where the origin of abandonment and forsakenness for the African Diaspora began. What is often forgotten is that inherent in their existence is the fact that the people of the African Diaspora share breath with the divine, which formed their souls in creation (Genesis 2:7). Forgetting the people share the breath of God allows that they may be viewed as evil. Forgetting when to inhale and exhale or hold one's breath that is shared with the divine includes the collective breath of the African Diaspora. The co-sufferer who understands has not forsaken or forgotten the breath shared with the African Diaspora. Thus, the problem of race links from breath to justice. Once it is assumed a being has no soul, evil can be perpetrated against that being.

Part III. Catching Our Breath

1. Breath Interrupted: An Introduction

Excuse me while I try to catch my breath! Cause breathing ain't easy in this strange land called America. I cannot catch my breath because the air is not clean. See, a lot of dirt's been done in America. When are we going to clean the air, America? When are we going to clear the air, America? Cause we have to secure future breath for our sons and daughters. And your highways and byways are polluted by a toxic legacy that permeates the atmosphere and interrupts breath—it's been far too long since my African ancestors arrived on these shores. Breath stolen. For they could not easily catch the breath that was being *sold. Taken. Stolen. Interrupted.*

Breath

By the waters of the Atlantic, breath was first interrupted. As interrupted black bodies sunk to the ocean's floor. *Breath sold, taken, stolen, interrupted,* and taken to a new land far from the distant shore. And the legacy of a people's breath being casually interrupted without cause begins in America. Breath casually being interrupted by nooses and knees. Another generation survives to tell the story, and we find that breath being interrupted, still? Breath interrupted as a memory of the not forgotten from great grandma to grandma, to momma, to me, we find breath interrupted by ballots and billy clubs. Still? Still.

We find breath causally and constantly being interrupted like a game of sport. A fool's game played by fools who control the rules of engagement in this great land called America. Breath interrupted, killing dreams of imagined futures that hold our democratic ideals for tomorrow's tortured souls of sons and daughters. *Breath sold, taken, stolen, interrupted.* For the senseless erasure of the beautiful black breath sold, taken, stolen out of this realm, we kindred folks will meet you in the next world where we will breathe uninterrupted. For displacement is breath interrupted. Dislocation is breath interrupted. Dispersal is breath interrupted. Erasure is breath interrupted. Genocide is breath interrupted. Colonization is breath interrupted. Enslavement is breath interrupted.

What say you, colonizer? What say you, enslaver? What say you, good white people? What say you, capitalist? What say you to a generation of survivors of anti-black violence and anti-black racism, of a people whose breath has been interrupted to build this great nation? How long? Too long. How do you defend the lack of democratic reforms around issues of voting rights, civil rights, human rights, and all the areas that interrupt the breath of black Americans? It seems as if the US Constitution, the Declaration of Independence, and all the social contracts that govern this land hold inherent in their mandates that every citizen has the right to live and breathe uninterrupted. But somehow, this fundamental human right has yet to be fully achieved by black American citizens.

A people's collective deep breath is even harder to catch when interrupted. In Tulsa, Oklahoma, in 1921, in a neighborhood

Breath | Voice | Fire

known as Black Wall Street, a group of black Americans breathed deeply. Independently. They had achieved for themselves the American Dream all on their own. Business owners, merchants, teachers, doctors, lawyers, skilled tradespeople, nurses, and farmers, with their collective breath, built a fantastic community before their breath was interrupted by genocide in the form of smoke. Breath for them was self-reliance. Breath for them was self-determination. Breath was not needing anyone or being dependent on anyone for anything. But breath was interrupted by sparks. Breath was interrupted by flames. Breath was interrupted by fire. Breath was interrupted, and then all that was left were ashes.

May 31, 2021, marked the hundredth anniversary of the Tulsa race massacre. In 2021, we remembered Tulsa, and we saw ghosts and glimpses of a little-known American tragedy as we walked through the ashes of communities burned after the deaths of black sons and daughters at the hands of an angry white mob. We honor the ancestors of the Black Wall Street massacre and all the other cases of anti-black violence—of breath interrupted—still. Tulsa is one example of *breath sold, taken, stolen, or interrupted*. Dramatic, horrific scenes of anti-black racism worked then.

How it works now is more methodical. Deliberate. As one traffic stop at a time. As one knee at a time vs. the dramatic burning down of an entire flourishing town all at once. Anti-black violence is the breath of a people interrupted. Breath interrupted until the cycle stops. Will anti-black violence end with this modern generation? Will anti-black racism continue to be perpetuated through American systems of governance? Will anti-black racism continue to be taught to innocent white children during their formative years as a ceremonial rite of passage and acceptance by the dominant culture?

The time to stop anti-black racism that interrupts black breath is now. No more interruptions of black breath. No more. Let us breathe uninterrupted. Please do not continue to interrupt our breath! For once, let us begin to breathe uninterrupted.

Breath

2. Breath and Masks

Who are black Americans unmasked? Breathing. Never missing one single breath. Black skin does not spend like white skin. White skin spends like currency. Flowing through this world unmasked and unashamed. Black Americans wear our masks because of the viruses that plague us, but wearing masks makes it extremely hard to breathe. After several long seasons of encounters with coronavirus and the virus of racism, one might ask, "Who are the people of the African Diaspora unmasked?" Who are we unveiled? Maskless. Are we then our authentic selves? What are these objects known as masks, and how have they dominated and controlled our lives?

From Frantz Fanon to W. E. B. Du Bois, we learn how masks have challenged our ability to breathe and live authentically. Masks shield us from unsafe places like restricted neighborhoods, college campuses, executive board rooms, country clubs, and the halls of government that rule this great nation. Masks that turn us into prisoners of ourselves as we are forced to face foreign self-images that sometimes make us unidentifiable to ourselves. Once masked, we hate the false selves we have created. But are we then able to breathe freely without our breath uninterrupted? Masked and inauthentic. That is the way of the world for black Americans.

We wear our masks proudly, and we wear our masks with shame, but more than that, we wear our masks to protect our breath. The masks we wear are for survival from the viruses that plague our lives. Our masks guard us against the brutal truth about our world and our place in it. We are not safe from the viruses that plague our world, so we must wear our masks.

Why do we wear masks? In a world of absurdity, we wear many masks. Masks of shrouded identity make a rancid world more palatable. Masks of illusion that reinterpret truth so the "Other" fits into boxed images and fantasies of inferiority. We wear masks for protection. We wear masks for belonging. We wear masks for integration. We wear masks for assimilation. We wear masks for minstrelsy (entertainment). We wear masks for acceptance. We wear masks for deliverance. We wear masks for safety. We wear masks for surrender. We wear masks for protection. We wear masks for resistance. We wear our masks in solidarity. We wear our masks in protest. Yes, we wear all these masks and more.

Black Americans, for the survival of our breath, it is demanded that we show up in this world masked. Always. Covered. Veiled. Hidden. As if the truth of who we are unmasked is simply just too much for our planet. But it ain't easy breathing through this mask! Identity suffocated. Life force cut off. Who are we unmasked? Historically, the oppressor has called us savages, barbarians, heathens, non-human, unredeemable, killable, different, other. Our identity suffocated behind assimilationist masks makes us like zombies stumbling through life as total impostors and caricatures. Black America's identity unmasked strikes fear in the hearts of those who refuse to see themselves in people like me.

Unmasked. Who we are unmasked is powerful. But instead, we mask our true identity. We mask our breath. We mask our intentions. We mask our fear. We mask our truth. We mask our power. We mask our beauty. We mask our pain. We mask our identity. We mask our authenticity. We mask our liberation. Most importantly, we mask our revolutionary moments to create change when we mask our breath.

The performance of blackness in America unmasked breathes freely. Effortlessly. And it allows us to be who we truly are. The children of God made us to be in the image of God. Breath masked suffocates the creative imagination. It stifles, chokes, and sanctions our best selves from being made manifest. We are masked for the sole comfort of others at the detriment of ourselves. Because there is nowhere black bodies can hide in this great nation and assume an identity separate from the social construction of blackness, we embrace blackness and the existential crisis we must overcome. And with breath unmasked, we breathe our world of blackness despite those who wish to capture our breath—the same breath we cannot catch for very long. Despite those who wish to silence our voice, we breathe our world of blackness. Despite those who wish to extinguish our fire, we breathe our world of blackness. And we breathe, and we breathe, and we breathe on. To rhythms set by our foremothers and forefathers that gave us the mask and the dance needed to perform lest we lose our breath! Lest we lose our voice! Lest we lose our fire! For our breath, voice, and fire not to be captured, silenced, or extinguished.

We dance masked and breathe to the heavens as we win the day. Dance and the breath supply remain. The mask of the dance is the ancestor's gift for the survival of unsuspecting generations who do not yet know evil. Sing, and the breath supply remains for the mask of the song, the ancestor's gift to unsuspecting generations who do not yet know evil.

Since 2020, the masks have been taking a heavy toll on black breath. Can't tell when the performance of blackness masked will ever end. Been so long that we've been told assimilationist fantasies of full inclusion in the American Dream. A heavy burden indeed, these masks. Breath constrained; we do our best to catch our breath while masked. We wear masks for the dance that is blackness in America. The dance of breath. The dance of survival to live and to breathe one more breath. One more generation basking in the sun's shadow. Until the day we all see God's face unmasked and the truth is revealed. We rise with the Spirit masked to dance and breathe one last dance before we see the face of God. *Breath, voice, and fire are the cosmic gifts of the ancestors passed on for our survival.*

3. Breath and Double Consciousness

"It is a peculiar sensation, this double-consciousness, this sense of always looking at oneself through the eyes of others, of measuring one's soul by the tape of a world that looks on in amused contempt and pity."[14]

—W. E. B. Du Bois

Black American identity exists in what W. E. B. Du Bois refers to as double consciousness. From the time black American children speak, we are taught that we have two different faces we share with

14. Du Bois, *Souls of Black Folk*, 2.

the world. These two faces represent our two separate identities. One identity takes on an assimilationist persona trained to perform the social behaviors found acceptable or respectable to the dominant society. The other identity is our authentic selves, the persona we perform primarily for our communities. This double consciousness results from the tenuous position we find ourselves in following the psychological horrors of slavery and Jim Crow laws.

This manner of black Americans occupying dual identities may seem absurd to some. To black Americans, it is a means of survival. Two faces for two Americas. One can imagine it as necessary a tool for survival for black Americans as anything. History has proven some of the merits of double consciousness. Historically, black Americans who do not fully understand the nuance of living in this dualistic reality are often met with the brutal, harsh realities of those who demand our obedience and assimilation.

As a means of survival, black boys are taught at an early age how to respond in a particular manner, tone, and tenor to law enforcement officers, including police, judges, state troopers, state prosecutors, correctional officers, and all officers of the court. One never knows when one will encounter a law enforcement officer or court officer with implicit bias against non-white citizens who appear before them. The philosophy of double consciousness allows the person being racially profiled to present a survivalist persona that is more amicable to law enforcement, thus resulting in a better outcome after the profiling exchange. Inherent in the alternate, survivalist persona exists the coping mechanisms needed to transcend the scenario of injustice now so one can live to see another day. Does this mean every black American's life will be spared while experiencing racial profiling? The answer is no. Anti-black violence is a natural phenomenon in America. However, through the double consciousness mindset, one can manage the crisis more clearly, thus offering better responses when the crisis arises.

Double consciousness allows us to catch our breath (sort of!). This mindset among black Americans will let us be who this country needs us to be, albeit momentarily. Double consciousness sometimes allows black Americans to avert an early demise.

Breath

Double consciousness reflects who the power structure needs us to be in this country. Historically, in this philosophy of double consciousness, some were saved from being lynched in the Jim Crow South. But not all. Emmett Till was a young boy who, for one moment, neglected to follow his mother Mamie's instructions to perform an acceptable version of himself while in the presence of white folks in the deep South.

With his breath and voice, young Emmett dared to speak freely one afternoon to a white woman in a town outside Money, Mississippi, in August 1955. Young Emmett was well taught about the social boundaries between the races. Originally from Chicago, he was only visiting his uncle down south. "Say yes, ma'am" or "Yes, sir!" "Keep your eyes down." "Never let your eyes meet those of a white person." "Put your money on the counter cause your hands can't touch." All these "manners" his mother taught him. In the heat of the moment, on a dare from one of the other local boys on the scene, Emmett courageously spoke freely from his authentic self, not his assimilationist self as his mother advised him, to a white woman working as a store clerk. As he misjudged and failed to assess the moment, young Emmett learned just how easily one's breath could be interrupted in an instant when refusing to perform the dualistic persona demanded and required of a black man in the Jim Crow South.

As the tragic life of Emmett Till foreshadows the life of George Floyd and many others, we recognize something frightening in the dualistic performance of the identity of blacks in America. Even when forced to give assimilationist versions of ourselves for our survival, there are no guarantees that we will not still lose our lives at the hands of law enforcement. At a maximum, that assimilationist performance offers a *chance* for one to survive. This lack of guarantee presents a flaw in the double consciousness philosophy.

It is time for us to move race relations beyond assimilation, double consciousness, and dualistic identities. For in our authenticity, we possess the power to create real change. Systemic change. Structural change. Revolutionary change. The philosophy of double consciousness had run its course in the narrative of black folks in America as we all watched George Floyd speaking calmly, respectfully, cautiously, and humbly (within the mindset of double consciousness) to law enforcement before he was choked to death before our eyes. The double-consciousness philosophy did not protect George Floyd's breath. It is time for a change.

4. Combat Breathing

> "There is no occupation of territory on the one hand and independence of person on the other. It is the country, its history, its daily pulsation that is contested, and disfigured in the hope of a final deconstruction. Under these conditions, the individual's breathing is an observed, an occupied breathing. It is a combat breathing."[15]
>
> —Frantz Fanon

> "We revolt simply because, for many reasons, we can no longer breathe."[16]
>
> —Frantz Fanon

At the height of the conflict in French colonial Algiers, philosopher Frantz Fanon described the phenomenon of combat breathing as follows: "Under these conditions, the individual's breathing is an observed, occupied breathing. It is a combat breathing."[17] Combat breathing is breath controlled or measured or breathing under a state of constant surveillance. In Fanon's example, we see the foundational issue that parallels with slow American genocide in the form of racial profiling and anti-black violence.

Black Americans in urban communities live in a modern-day police state. Every action is carefully monitored and surveilled. In the face of recent discussions around police reform, we have been reminded of Fanon's legacy that teaches the philosophy of combat breathing to understand our racialized world following the

15. Fanon, *Dying Colonialism*, 65.
16. Fanon, *Black Skins, White Masks*, 201.
17. Fanon, *Black Skins, White Masks*, 201.

current wave of black Americans who have died in police custody. One can conclude that black Americans instinctively understand the Fanonian concept of combat breathing. So, what is "occupied breathing"[18] in the Fanonian context?

One could say it is a way of controlling the breath. Occupied breathing or a breath controlled is an oxymoron as breath symbolizes man's freedom more than any other notion one can fathom. The state's desire and ability to control who breathes and does not is a familiar trope in the American narrative. Who lives and who does not? Whose life has worth, and whose does not? Which neighborhoods should be targeted for aggressive community policing, and which should be left alone and in peace? Which children get the best education, and which get an inferior one? Who gets to be the haves, and who gets to be the have-nots? Who gets to be incarcerated, and who gets a slap on the wrist in the form of community service? Who gets to breathe, and who gets a knee or a noose?

Combat breathing can also be interpreted as a response to unreasonable conditions. Fanon stated, "When we revolt it is not for a particular culture. We revolt simply because, for many reasons, we can no longer breathe."[19] Since 1619, black Americans have had to fight for the right to breathe. Since our first days on American soil, our breath has been scrutinized. Since the murders of George Floyd and countless others, the entire world has had the opportunity to witness and participate with black Americans protesting not so much as a revolt but as resistance to anti-black violence. To reiterate the words of Fanon, "We revolt simply because, for many reasons, we can no longer breathe."[20] In the case of black American sons and daughters, we do not revolt in the Fanonian sense, but we resist. As we allow our breath to become the weapons of resistance in an occupied state of America, we live to see another day. Our response to combat breathing, controlled and occupied, is a weaponized breath against state forces that eliminate non-white, "less

18. Fanon, *Black Skins, White Masks*, 201.
19. Fanon, *Black Skins, White Masks*, 201.
20. Fanon, *Black Skins, White Masks*, 201.

desirable" citizens who can no longer breathe normally. We have worked through the conditions that forced combat breathing, controlled and occupied, as an attempt to gain independence from the American power structure, its program of racial profiling, and the terrorism of a police state. As racial profiling creates the conditions of war in the form of a police state in urban communities across this nation, we learn that breath = independence.

Modern community policing statutes currently on the books are merely warmed-over statutes from the Jim Crow laws meant to control the movements of chattel enslaved people and protect the private property of white citizens at any cost. Most police departments in America have not amended these state laws, thus allowing the penal system to unjustly target black people through forced combat breathing or controlled and occupied breath. Today's mass incarceration system is designed for and filled with black people through forced combat breathing or controlled and occupied breath. Racial profiling is the legal tool that allows black bodies to be collected for jails to be filled through forced combat breathing or controlled and occupied breath. Thus satisfying a billion-dollar prison industrial complex. Racial profiling creates the conditions of a police state as it simultaneously creates profits.

Those who do not become incarcerated too often die at the hands of the police. Black communities can no longer breathe because their breath has been interrupted by the police state's mandates on profiling to meet arrest quotas. This "observed" and "occupied" breathing we have witnessed most recently has shaken America's image as millions questioned everything they thought they knew about law enforcement in this country after the death of George Floyd. A few bad apples or neglected police reform for too long? You decide. Why are modern police stations still using legal statutes for community policing that enforce antiquated slave codes from centuries ago? Not sure why? But the reality is that black Americans must fight for the right to breathe independently, not surveilled by the state. As black Americans gain our independence, as we catch our breath, we become who we are meant to be authentically.

Breath

Part IV. Black Feminist/Womanist Breath

> "somebody/anybody, sing a black girl's song . . .
> she's been dead so long, closed in silence so long,
> she doesn't know the sound of her own voice."
>
> —NTOZAKE SHANGE, *FOR COLORED GIRLS*[21]

1. Catching Our Breath at the Intersection of Race, Class, and Gender

> "Say her name!"
>
> —IN HONOR OF BREONNA TAYLOR

> "I breathe, therefore I am."[22]
>
> —LUCE IRIGARAY

> "There can be no love without justice.
> Without justice, there can be no love."[23]
>
> —BELL HOOKS

Black feminine breath does not breathe easily. Dominated by the patriarchal power structure and often existing on the margins, black feminine breath resists the color line, the glass ceiling, voter suppression, equal pay discrimination, and economic exploitation to safeguard democracy and help create a more perfect union. We already know that black breath is hard to catch and is easily lost. But for those who reside in black female bodies, the primary task of breathing takes on another dimension of complexity, as a black feminine breath has the peculiar responsibility of safeguarding American democracy. The dilemma around

---

21. Shange, *For Colored Girls*, 17–19.
22. Quoted in Škof, *Breath of Proximity*, 130.
23. hooks, *All About Love*, 19.

black feminine breath then becomes its inherent intersectionality as it has the burden of working to secure democracy for future generations of sons and daughters.

How does one catch one's breath in the face of racism, classism, and sexism? This act of breathing should be a God-given human right by all standard accounts. However, black feminine breath is contested as it challenges the continuity of patriarchy. Catching one's breath represents a means of survival in a patriarchal system resistant to change. Black feminine breath has struggled against oppression and expanded our ideas of inclusion for all-in health care advocacy and many other forms of progressive democracy. Black feminine breath leads the moral discourse and serves as an agent of radical social change in economics, capitalism, and politics during these turbulent times.

What then is the existential crisis for black feminine breath? Why can't black feminine breath breathe easily? Why isn't existence alone enough to justify black feminine breath's reason for being? Because of the presence of domination and marginalization presented by the patriarchy, black feminine bodies exist in an oppositional role within society, which shifts what is normative or what is reality. For black feminine breath existing on the margins, it is not as simple as declaring the Western reality, "I breathe therefore I am." In response to Luce Irigaray's statement, "I breathe therefore I am," I would say, not always. No matter what everyone else is doing, one cannot assume that black feminine breath is breathing easily on the margins. bell hooks wrote,

> Living as we did, on the edge, we developed a particular way of seeing reality. We looked both from the outside in and from the inside out. We focused our attention on the center as well as on the margin. We understood both. This mode of seeing reminded us of the existence of a whole universe, the main body made up of both margin and center. Our survival depended on an ongoing public awareness of the separation between margin and center and an ongoing private acknowledgment that we were a necessary, vital part of that whole. This sense of wholeness, impressed upon our consciousness by the structure

Breath

of our daily lives, provided us with an oppositional world-view—a mode of seeing unknown to most of our oppressors that sustained us, aided us in our struggle to transcend poverty and despair, strengthening our sense of self and our solidarity.[24]

hooks's philosophies centered black women's ideas as part of the literary activism that defined her work. This is the work in the public square right now as black women's activism, organizing, and political leadership have expanded the national discourse by centering the experiences of black women's voices to lead major social movements of our day. From a historical standpoint, black women's activism in America spans over 200 years. It includes fearless women like Harriet Tubman, Sojourner Truth, Rosa Parks, Fannie Lou Hamer, Ella Baker, Ida B. Wells, and Angela Davis. We must say their names as we witness their sacred breath through their work. As for our recent times, three black women—Alicia Garza, Patrisse Khan-Cullors, and Opal Tometi—founded the Black Lives Matter movement.

bell hooks knew that black women's perspectives were necessary because of our depth of perception from working from the margins. hooks brought black women's particularism to feminist discourse. After Kimberlé Crenshaw introduced intersectionality in 1989, hooks built on the concept and taught us the importance of understanding American society through the lived experiences of black women (via the intersectionality of race, class, and gender). The expansion of intersectionality as a movement within feminism gave black women a moment to become central in discussions of power and inclusion. Crenshaw defines intersectionality as "a framework to understand the interconnected nature of social and political identities and how these create interdependent systems of discrimination, a 'many-layered blanket of oppression.'"[25] This theory of intersectionality demonstrates the value of black women's experiences that need to be more visible to help us reshape the white male power structure.

24. hooks, *Feminist Theory*, xvi.
25. Quoted in Baldwin, "bell hooks and the growth of intersectionality."

Breath | Voice | Fire

In an unjust world, there is music
For the soul to resist the unfathomable
In the somber voices of
Black women who sing our stories
Black women who embody God
Like Zora Neale Hurston
Toni Morrison
Alice Walker
Through them, we learn that we are
Undiminished human beings
Made in the image of God
With only song beating in our hearts
We remember those times
When we were whole
—Sharon Kimberly Williams

Original Poems and Poetics on Breath

"In the beginning, God created heaven and earth. And the earth was without form and void, and darkness was upon the face of the deep. And the Spirit [breath or ruach] of God moved upon the face of the waters."

—Genesis 1:1

"Breath is the bridge which connects life to consciousness, which unites your body to your thoughts. Whenever your mind becomes scattered, use your breath as the means to take hold of your mind again."[26]

—Thich Nhat Hanh

What is the connection between the body, breath, healing, and holistic health in African cosmology and epistemology? Breath bridges our inner and outer worlds. Breath engages spirit, mind, and body. The performance of our lives constantly engages the rituals of breath and breathing to honor the body, centering it, and aligning it with wholeness. Spirituals, blues, jazz, hip-hop. These

---

26. Hahn, *Miracle of Mindfulness*, 15.

rituals of song allow us to practice capturing that which was stolen. Catching our breath in performance is the ritual of reclaiming through song and will enable us to create a worldview that imagines our bodies in states of wholeness through a breath that creates balance. Breath is what integrates the mind, body, and spirit and recognizes the sacredness of lives that matter.

I. Breath as a Bridge Between Our Interior to the Exterior World

Breathe, lest we forget our source! What can be found in the memory of breath? In cosmic breath brought forth from a distant time before the creation of the world, one can find a bridge. As we remember our breath, we recognize that a bridge connects our spirit's home to our conscious mind. From the ancient breath that once vibrated upon the face of the deep, the bridge that is breath remembers our creation and what it means to be liberated and free.

Like a wind, breath whispered to announce the coming of liberation from suffering. Breath is the bridge between the spirit world and the natural world. Breath is the bridge between sickness and health. Breath is the bridge between the living and the dead. Breath is the bridge between emptiness and fullness. Breath is the bridge between the spirit and the body. Breath is the bridge between the body and the mind—breath is a bridge between mind and spirit. Breath is the Spirit that bridges and interconnects all beings and bridges our interior and exterior worlds.

How does breath bridge our interior and exterior world, and why does the relationality of breath matter in the study of mindfulness and spirituality? This interconnectedness of our inner and outer worlds is bridged together by the energy of the cosmic pathway, also known as breath. The quality of attention we pay to our breath puts us in touch with our conscious mind. As we grow more conscious of our breath, we become more conscious of our interconnectedness with all creation. It is breath that animates our human form into being. My following poems explore these truths.

Breath | Voice | Fire

Rhythm of Breath: An Exodus Poetics of Becoming

All throughout the African Diaspora
the Spirit is manifest
as an exodus of human souls
dispersed the world around
with a common purpose
carrying a certain rhythm
in the souls of the people
A uniquely syncopated African breath that is
simultaneously
individual and collective
Black, African, Caribbean, Afro-Latino
An exodus rhythm of
dislocation, displacement, dispersal, exile
sometimes erasure—not often return—
a syncopated cycle
of breath for the African Diaspora

What happens when the rhythm is disrupted?
Keeping in time with the rhythm
of exodus is essential breath
for an African Diaspora whose
survival depends on
keeping faith
with this rhythm
which dictates the
movement of a people
through a wilderness toward *becoming*
more divine after
being dehumanized

Breath

We keep with the rhythm lest the cycle stop!
Wisdom chooses to keep time
with the rhythm of this world order
which was predestined by the colonizers
when they decided
who will be "the first"?
who will be "the last"?
For Black bodies, for "the last,"
who refuses to be dislocated?
the cycle stops at erasure

What does this movement reveal?
What revelation does it conceal?
Could we ever divine its divine purpose?

Perhaps it is the colossal dislocation
of the African Diaspora
that will in time create
a sustained, stabilizing
rhythm for all of humanity

But at what cost?
But at what cost?

Breath | Voice | Fire

Africana Spirit of Breath, Voice & Fire

Breathe, Africana people!
Lest you forget your source,
Forgotten breath casts a shadow on the memory.

For a dispersed people destined,
To sing in the stranger's land,
Who else but the Spirit will teach you your song?

Remember the ancestral voice that penetrates the silence,
Like a fire shut up in the valley of dry bones,
Let Spirit move on the Diaspora's sons and daughters.

Remember the ancestors, and don't forget your breath,
Remember the ancestors, and don't forget your voice,
Remember the ancestors, and don't forget your fire!

This is your Spirit song.—Selah.

Breath

We Ain't Afraid to Sing Our World

I'd like to teach the world to sing
In perfect harmony
So, then I am lyric, rhythm,
The Dissonance Within
Is the Sultry sound of
Global soul,
We Africana people
We ain't afraid to sing a world
Nurtured from the root
With rhizomes that heal
For radical health
We be made well
By the dissonance
Of lamented souls
Remembered in song
Rescued from abandonment
Never forgotten or forsaken
In those hollow bellies
Resides a hunger
That rumbles in harmony
Rejecting man's inhumanity to man
With all the unnecessary evils
And elevate haunted voices with
Deep connection
Sound sinews
Shut up in the marrow of our bones
No.
We ain't afraid to sing our world!

Breath of Lyric

1. sweet syntax
2. woven into worlds
3. arranging the matters of the
4. heart and mind and soul and Spirit
5. into a captive secret
6. like a tapestry of language
7. spoken only by the muse
8. your words seal us
9. simultaneously
10. into uncertainty and safety
11. like a familiar melody
12. harkening to a distant refrain
13. your truth gives sound as a
14. blessed assuredness
15. to birth stories into
16. sacredness
17. that deliver us from
18. the forgottenness of time stolen
19. by teaching survival from
20. the inevitability of
21. oppression

Breath

22. domination, dominion
23. image that?
24. same words, different woman
25. same words, different man
26. how do you write our varied lives?
27. so eloquently yet tragically and then
28. deliver us
29. into the hidden
30. beauty
31. of forgotten places
32. near ancient shores
33. we try to keep pace
34. with your rhythm
35. in time
36. to restore our memory
37. of precious things
38. carelessly forgotten
39. we keep pace
40. to gain something greater
41. than it ever was or ever could be
42. you imagine better
43. I just remember getting lost
44. inside the melody and
45. what I found was my best and that
46. you alone make life
47. beautiful

Breath | Voice | Fire

Breath of Life: Imago Dei

Teacher, can you birth me?
Breathe life into me?
I come as an embryo
Needing to be born
into an uncertain existence

which requires so much more
than our small, biased minds can
fathom to
comprehend

entangled humans
we connect at every seam
with invisible strands like lifelines
infinitely imagined
why create human beings
in your sacred image
and make them so different
from you, from each other

for you to be you
I have to be me
reflecting humanity
onto each other's otherness

hollowed out souls
seeking to find
the perfect image of perfection
in a world of flaws

Breath

co-creation and co-imagination
connects humans and the divine
sparking the chaos
between the two worlds

the duality instead reflects
the divinity in flesh
your truth revealed
to teach humanity

human to human
human to divine
like two visions of the same bond
we are not so different

Breath | Voice | Fire

This is MAGA Country?

This is MAGA country?
What makes it yours?
Is it your perfected hatred of God's creation?
Or your appetite for dominion over difference?
Is it your insatiable hunger for a random act of rage?
Starving for the privilege of absolute power,
Like an all-consuming, entitling birthright,
That makes you want to rule with the power of an empire over the "Other,"
And stirs up the sleeping violence deeply embedded in your soul,
What you think of Black skin,
Doesn't change one damn thing,
Cleanse the heart instead,
Of the one who prepares,
A noose fitted for Black necks,
Coincidently??
Not guilty of anything more,
Than being,
Than being who God made him be,
Than loving who he loves,
Than breathing contested air,
In a land that may not be his,
Perhaps this land is MAGA land,
It is God, not the MAGA empire,
That will reign supreme.

Breath

Mirroring Breath

Who summoned her?
Is there a revolutionary in my mirror?
If so, when, how, and why?
If so, where did she come from?
Did she wake from a deep slumber?
Like the hibernating history
of anti-Black violence
Repeating itself
Is she destined for a time like this?
Or is it just that
someone must prepare for revolution
when it's inevitable?
Still, what I see in that mirror
could be right or wrong
All that matters is
who woke her?
Who called her forth?
And for what purpose?
Is it time to stay woke?
Or to continue the dream
that is destined to end
as a nightmare?

Chapter Two

Voice

Nobody knows the trouble I've seen
Nobody knows my sorrow
Nobody knows the trouble I've seen
Glory hallelujah!

Sometimes I'm up,
Sometimes I'm down
Oh, yes, Lord
Sometimes I'm almost to the ground
Oh, yes, Lord

Nobody knows the trouble I've seen
Nobody knows but Jesus
Nobody knows the trouble I've seen
Glory hallelujah!

—NEGRO SPIRITUAL

Voice

Part I: A Letter to America

Dear America,

Beloved, there is trouble in the land.

Troubles are passed down from generation to generation. From the colonizer to the colonized and the slave owner to the slave. To you and me. The powerful and the powerless alike. Like a carnival trophy in a game of chance, the legacy of bondage is a paradoxical prize nobody wants to win. In this way, you are the trouble, and the trouble is you. This inheritance of trouble, or a troubled people, becomes your birthright where all of the nation's troubles can be blamed upon dark-skinned kin. When one's race is "the trouble," this perspective of being "the trouble or troubled" permeates the identity of a person.

One is blamed for their socially constructed (human-made, not God-ordained) racial assignment, and one's life becomes "a race" to conquer the problem of "one's race" (race being a fabricated social construction that has no true merit, as there is only one true race, the human race). Yet race becomes how one and one's people are described. How one and one's people are known to the world. *Troubled.* As it is written in the Negro spiritual quoted at the top of this chapter, "Nobody knows the trouble I've seen. Nobody knows our sorrow." This is the challenge for the descendants of enslaved Africans living in America today.

Likewise, one will also know the oppressor by his troubles and by his sorrows. For he sows trouble for the oppressed throughout the generations. He has consistently written trouble into the laws of this nation against the human and civil rights of its non-white citizens. Oppressive laws of the past are currently being upheld by the oppressor's offspring today. In the book of Isaiah, it is written, "Woe to those who make unjust laws, to those who issue oppressive decrees, to deprive the poor of their rights and withhold justice from the oppressed of my people." Oppressive laws work against American democracy and the fundamental notions of humanity.

In the paradox of the enslaved Africans' legacy of trouble on the United States shores lies the truth, America, of who you are. The trouble you have distributed on the backs of your black sisters and brothers tells a troubled story of hatred. From slavery to Jim Crow in the land of the free and the home of the brave, the hypocrisy of freedom and liberty is how you will be known to the world as the remnants of segregated laws are still alive and well today in American housing, education, and criminal justice systems (just to name a few). The trouble of racially motivated chaos and catastrophe in America turns otherwise good men and women into monsters.

This is what you become, America, as you secretly sing, "Nobody knows the trouble I've seen. Nobody knows my sorrows." The burden of maintaining racial hierarchy through hateful systems of white supremacy and the work it entails to ensure a segregated society across generations is often too much to bear. This notion of two Americas and the dualistic identity juxtaposed to the notion of America as a white, Christian nation is what threatens to divide and tear this diverse country apart. Systems of white supremacy demand too much of one's soul. And the rise of white supremacy is the real trouble America continues to remain silent about. Generation after generation, the acknowledgment of white supremacy in America can be fearful. We know the trouble you've seen. We know your sorrows. We know the burden one must bear through the reality of our tethered connection to this land. A near genocide of indigenous Americans. Turning free men into slaves. Depriving men and women of their God-given rights to liberty. What does all of this cost, America?

As both slave and slave master share in the legacy of trouble as written in the "Nobody knows" lament, know that the oppression one serves upon one's neighbor is also served upon oneself. To enslave makes one a slave. Like the old parable, "When one digs a grave, better dig two!" For the slave master, the work of dehumanizing human beings created in the image of God has bound the people to one of the worst chapters in world history. How much work does it take to be the oppressor and to make corrupt systems that operate against God's natural law? How much of a toll does oppression take on one's soul?

Voice

Nobody knows, you say. Your troubles and our troubles, entangled as they are, are different troubles with a shared root. American roots unveiled are divided and can easily be measured in black and white, tethered together and *both* troubled for sure. Southern strategies rob both groups of people, and keep America from reaching its full potential as a nation. The American story is a story of empire and power. And America's troubles are rooted in the trouble of racial hierarchies and racialized subjugation. How do some think and believe their humanity is worth more than others when we were all created in the image of God?

For those who are still deeply against full integration and social equality of the races today, therein lies the source of the sickness in our hearts as the trouble of white supremacy lay dormant in the heart of a nation. Silent. Hidden in plain sight and liberated. No longer in the secret places. Untouched by truth, each season it waits patiently for the opportunity to resurface. Not fully revealing itself. Only proclaiming a hatred. No one can know the depths of America's pain and sorrow. Nobody knows the cost of American exceptionalism and the dark secrets hidden in the lie of it as a young democracy still struggles to live up to the basic tenets of its creed.

Too many Americans are lamenting, "Nobody knows the trouble I've seen." If we could only deal with the root cause of our sorrows and stop hiding the truth behind our troubles, America. Perhaps then America could begin to heal itself from its true illness, which is rooted in the false narratives of superiority and inferiority among the races.

> *Over my head I see trouble in the air,*
> *Over my head I see trouble in the air,*
> *Over my head I see trouble in the air,*
> *There must be a God somewhere.*

> *Oh, when the world is silent,*
> *I hear music in the air,*
> *Oh, when the world is silent,*

Breath | Voice | Fire

I hear music in the air,
Oh, when the world is silent,
I hear music in the air,
There must be a God somewhere.

—Negro Spiritual

Beloved, there is trouble in the air

In his 1968 speech "Remaining Awake Through a Great Revolution," Dr. Martin Luther King Jr. stated, "We shall overcome because the arc of the moral universe is long, but it bends toward justice."[1] As we begin to understand that the future of American democracy depends upon our ability to bend our universe—our American narrative—toward justice, this generation must understand it has upon its shoulders the very challenge of securing American democracy. America, do you understand just how much *trouble is in the air?* As we face the urgency of the moment, one could ask, *"What if good Americans remain silent on the issue of racism in America?"* To echo the words of the opening spiritual, "When the world is silent, there is often *trouble in the air."*

This generation knows a few things: The time for our nation to break its collective silence on anti-black racism is now. The time for our nation to raise its voice in defense of American democracy and our shared democratic ideals is now. But what will it cost America to be America? As America reluctantly deals with its diabolical legacy of racism, one must acknowledge that this nation needs a rebuke and a reckoning for this sin against humanity. Compassionately, America also needs reconciliation, redemption, and reparation so the nation can heal.

William Falkner taught us well about American history's time-space continuum when he wrote, "The past is never dead. It's not

---

1. King Jr., "Remaining Awake Through a Great Revolution."

even past."[2] From our nation's history, one learns the early American settlers spanned north to south and east to west. Traveling through the wilderness of American colonies and territories of a new nation soon to be born, one could ask, "But at what cost?" As the settlers conquered the land and enslaved others to work it, the ancestors stand united as they offer a rebuke for what happened on this land. Those early encounters with the English settlers ended in either death or enslavement for the ancestors. And for their unreconciled death and enslavement without proper acknowledgment of the historical record, *America, there will be a reckoning.*

From this perspective, one learns that America's past is bridged to its present in ways that inform our future. In other words, what happened in the past influences the future. Within this dimension of time and space, we hold in our hearts a hope for redemption, reconciliation, and healing for America's past as a way of securing its present and its future. By the ancestors' account, America's sin of racism is so grievous that redemption and reconciliation may only be able to occur following rebuke and a reckoning.

Thus, we need to imagine a transformational, transcendent finale for this American saga on the issue of race. We need a conclusion on the question of race in America that brings this country's cryptic historical narrative to its final crescendo. We need a conclusion on race that begins with good people breaking their silence on America's original sin and ends with America healed with a new identity as a post-racial society.

The time for America to deal with the cancer of racism is now. The recent emergence of outbursts of anti-black violence amidst the backdrop of a raging global pandemic forced our nation to bear a collective witness to racial disparities in the American health care system. Our youth began to chant, "Black Lives Matter" to explain their understanding of American systems, not designed for the betterment of all, but for a privileged few. From the past to the present to the future, if it takes a reckoning for America to understand this basic human truth, so be it. *Because Black Lives Matter!*

---

2. Falkner, *Requiem for a Nun*, 73.

Breath | Voice | Fire

There's trouble in the air! One of my favorite prophetic voices is that of James Baldwin. In 1954, Baldwin warned us of things to come when he penned *Notes of a Native Son*, and he stated, "The world is white no more."[3] This insightful line that ends the closing chapter of *Notes of a Native Son* speaks directly to our current times. Do we not feel the truth of this paradox as America's most privileged sons and daughters fight for their right to remain "white" after the world has changed as Baldwin suggested?

In 2008 during Barak Obama's presidential campaign, the United States Census reported that in 2042, non-Hispanic whites would be outnumbered by the aggregated population of all non-white citizens, which includes Hispanics, Blacks, Asians, Indigenous Americans, and Pacific Islanders.[4] And it is this exact point, more than anything, that marks the spirit of these turbulent times. The installment of the first black president and the warning of a white minority in America contributed to the surge in racial tension for all minority groups and a backlash of anti-black violence. We are living in fearful, troubled times indeed.

What happens when whiteness begins to shift from the center of the American consciousness? Will America still be America, then? Maybe not for some. What will become of whiteness when the white monopoly on America and claims of privilege over all other ethnic groups ends? Baldwin gives us some insight into these questions as he writes brilliantly about the fact that there is a "stranger who will not always be strange to this village."[5] Times change. What always was will not always be. America is changing. America is browning at a staggering rate. The strange, non-white "other" in your community may not be so strange to this land much longer. In this revelation from Baldwin, we know now what Baldwin knew then, which is best stated in the words of poet

---

3. Baldwin, *Collected Essays*, 129.
4. Prewitt, "Why the Announcement of a Looming White Minority."
5. Baldwin, *Collected Essays*, 129.

Voice

Langston Hughes when he wrote during the Harlem Renaissance, "I am the darker brother . . . I, too, am America!"[6] We know today that black people are American brothers and sisters, not strangers to this land. Because of voices like Baldwin and Hughes, today, in some small ways, black Americans are beginning to sit at the table. In the words of Hughes, "We have been kept in the kitchen long enough. We have grown and we are strong."[7] But there is still more work to be done.

There is trouble in the air. We have stumbled into a season in this American experiment when for the first time we can see this great nation is in jeopardy of falling prey to authoritarian forces that can permanently overturn our democratic system of government and permanently install a tyrannical government. Yes, *there was trouble in the air* in America when on January 6 of 2021, a violent mob of so-called "American Patriots," under the direction of the commander-in-chief, Donald J. Trump, stormed the United States Capitol in a failed attempt to reclaim the White House after losing the presidential election. When the threat of insurrection is on the rise, *there is trouble in the air*. It is not some of us, but all of us American citizens, black and white, who need to do precisely what mystic activist Catherine of Siena suggests when she stated, "Speak the truth in a million voices. It is silence that kills."[8] Beloved, do not let silence kill American democracy.

That is our call to action today: To speak the truth in a million voices. That means we must all use our collective voices in defense of American democracy. Together our voices create a tapestry of truth that protects America's fragile democracy from the grips of authoritarian forces. We now live in a time when it is commonplace for immoral things that occur in this country to be ignored. It is commonplace for government officials to conspire with domestic terrorists to rally behind white nationalist/white supremacist agendas. It is commonplace for anti-black violence to be propagated by officers when racially profiled people are taken

---

6. Hughes, "I, Too."
7. Hughes, "I, Too."
8. Catherine of Siena, cited by Dominican Sisters of Peace Missions.

into police custody. It is commonplace to ignore racial disparities in health care during the worst global pandemic in a hundred years. It is commonplace to allow black morbidity rates due to COVID-19 to skyrocket without recourse for those who do not have adequate access to health care.

There is trouble in the air. It is time for everyone no matter their privileged station in American society to raise their voices in solidarity with the movement developed to protect the sanctity of black sacred lives. Sacred, why? This phrase "black sacred lives" is not intended to incite the reactionary response of "all lives matter" or "blue lives matter" or deny whites or any other ethnic minority group their full humanity. That would only inflict on others the same injury that has been perpetrated against black Americans.

Acknowledging black lives as sacred is simply a reminder. It is an acknowledgment to the world of the sacred yet forgotten connection the sons and daughters of enslaved Africans have to this great land. Along with Indigenous or Native Americans, black lives should always be deemed sacred in the country where whiteness and white supremacy rule the day without memory or consideration for all those souls who made the American experiment possible. The ancestors of enslaved Africans and Native Americans bear witness to this fact and their spirits are the impetus for this writing today. I write this rebuke of America and its original sin as a descendant of enslaved Africans from West Africa. But it is only through the ancestral spirit guiding this work that the whole truth about America will unfold.

America owes an additional debt to the Indigenous Americans who lost their land. As the enslaved Africans worked on this stolen land for centuries, America's unsettled debt to both the original people native to this land and those who worked the land without the benefit of wages is at the core of the nation's current problems. America, this unsettled debt is what foreshadows the dismantling of this bloodstained democracy. The blood of enslaved Africans and indigenous Americans has soaked the soil of this land. From the Great Migration to the Trail of Tears, from the East Coast to the West Coast, from the northern to the southern border, the blood of the oppressed is stained on the bill, America. To the sons and daughters of this country's European forefathers who speak of this country as "theirs," I offer the words of W. E. B. Du Bois, who wrote, "Your country? How did it become yours? Before the Pilgrims landed, we were here."[9]

The enslaved African and indigenous American ancestors have a different understanding about who is justified in staking claim to America. And because of the unresolved issue of America's original sin, *there is trouble in the air* in the form of revolution. That is a revolution not of weapons and arms, but ideas rooted in moral leadership and inclusive government. A moral revolution of ideas is what is most needed to reshape this nation from top to bottom and dismantle the social construction of white supremacy. It is time for America to realize that it does not need the binary system of white against black for this nation to prosper.

It is time for white privilege to be decentered from the American identity. The anti-democratic power structure that functions under absurd notions of the supremacy and superiority of some and the inferiority of others must end, if again, for no other reason but to preserve the union. In the imaginative words inspired by the literary canon of James Baldwin, "I am not your Negro."[10] How long does whiteness need to rely on the crutch of the trope of the inferior Negro upon which the entire Western worldview and Western cultural identity have been built? This inferiority theory has been disproven repeatedly across the academic disciplines of biology, genetics, and religion for centuries. Yet here we are even now, chanting "Black Lives Matter" as if it were still 1968 or 1864.

Oh yes. There is trouble in the air! Consider the absurdity of the fact that an entire social movement had to be created to proclaim the fact that Black Lives Matter, in response to racial profiling and over-policing. This fact says more about America's violent, racist tendencies than most things in this country's checkered history. To be clear, a social movement, Black Lives Matter, had to be created to proclaim what would be obvious in most other places

---

9. Du Bois, *Souls of Black Folk*, 162.
10. Baldwin, *I Am Not Your Negro*.

around the world. But here in America, because of its legacy of white supremacy, we must constantly affirm black humanity and proclaim what should not ever need to be spoken.

Initially, most Americans did not understand the rationale for the Black Lives Matter movement. Many thought it was absurd for people of color to rally around this movement, chanting about how their lives mattered as if it were not understood that we are all the children of God made in the image of God. To whites, this must have seemed absurd. But the question today is how long are black bodies to be killed in the streets while other good Americans sit in silence? Beloved, it is the silence that is absurd, not the rallying cry in response to the importance of preserving black lives. Hear again the voice of the spiritual that says, "Over my head, there is trouble in the air. When the world is silent, I hear music in the air. There must be a God somewhere."[11] Check your silence, America.

In 2020, George Floyd's absurd murder at the hands of law enforcement went viral, and for a moment the silence was broken. To the sons and daughters of the enslaved Africans, that moment of broken silence can be likened to the transcendent, transformational music in the air of the spiritual. For a moment it was like a new song for a new day. We witnessed white Americans in record numbers marching hand in hand with black Americans in protest of the public murder of George Floyd. Finally, America was forced to see itself as it is in reality, not the ideal of what America aspires to be. The silence was broken, albeit briefly. The sons and daughters of enslaved Africans did proclaim, "There must be a God somewhere."

Still, there is trouble in the air. But fret not, beloved! The renowned civil rights activist John Lewis, who marched with Dr. King, stopped by on his journey for a while to teach us that the universe also bends toward "good trouble," which is good news today. John Lewis taught us and taught us well this moral principle, "When you see something that is not right, not fair, not just, you have a moral obligation, a mission, and a mandate, to stand up, to speak up, and speak out, and get in the way, get in trouble, good

---

11. "Over My Head."

trouble, necessary trouble."[12] As we examine the life and work of our dearly departed brother John Lewis, we know one thing for sure: There must be a God somewhere because John Lewis faced death so many times it was a miracle that he survived the civil rights movement.

With this assurance, go boldly into the world, beloved, and find good trouble everywhere you go. Those who will get into good trouble are the ones who will use their voices consciously for restorative justice in their communities. Those who will get into good trouble will break the silence that shields anti-black racism. Those who will get into good trouble will challenge the unjust laws and statutes that prevent America from being genuinely great and living up to its fullest potential. In the passing of this great soldier for justice, John Lewis, we echo again William Falkner's words, "The past is never dead. It's not even past." The civil rights movement is not dead; it continues today and expands itself through the voices of our youth who are the future. And the fight for the Voting Rights Act that marks Brother Lewis's congressional legacy is not dead; it continues today. And the voice of Brother Lewis is not dead; it continues today as a constant reminder to us of our mandate to use our voices as we navigate through our lives, never shying away from "good trouble, necessary trouble."

> "Speak up, speak out. Get into what I call Good trouble. Necessary trouble. Do what is right."
>
> —JOHN LEWIS

Good Trouble, Necessary Trouble: Social Activist Training for a New Generation

It is said in the book of Job, "Man that is born of a woman is of few days and full of trouble." Therefore, if one must have trouble, choose the path of good and necessary trouble. John Lewis gave us the blueprint of how to be an activist during his involvement in

---

12. CBS Mornings, "Note to Self."

the civil rights movement. As an activist, he was beaten, bloodied, arrested, and jailed forty-five times throughout his life.

Lewis's activism began at the age of fifteen in 1955. He faced death on numerous occasions for marching and standing up for the human and civil rights of all citizens. He used his voice during one of the most turbulent times in our nation's history. So where are the John Lewises of today? Will we wake up one day in the near future and find our democracy completely dismantled because too many good people sat in silence?

While growing up in Troy, Alabama, John Lewis would see Jim Crow signs, "Whites Only," and his mother would urge him, "Don't get in the way. That's just the way things are. Don't get into trouble." But later Rosa Parks and Dr. King inspired him to get into trouble by working to end segregation in America. As a child, Lewis wanted to be a preacher, so he practiced using his voice and honing his craft by preaching to the chickens. One day Lewis wrote to Dr. King because he knew his life was bigger than his daily reality of a simple life on the farm. "The boy from Troy," Dr. King would call him. Lewis studied in Nashville with a focus on the philosophies of peace and nonviolence.

A Road Map for Nonviolent Revolution

During his studies, John Lewis learned to never engage in violence. The highest moral values were instilled in him, and he always knew he had the right to protest for what was right. Civil rights activist Rev. James Lawson Jr. taught Lewis and others that nonviolence as conceived by the Montgomery Bus Boycott of 1956 was not a self-defense position. It was a militant position designed to empower his students to change their environments. The Montgomery Bus Boycott helped to wake the nation to its race problems. Lewis noted, "When you sit down on the bus and you sit down in the front, or you sit down by a white person, you have a duty to sit there because as long as you sit in the back, you have a false sense of inferiority and so as long as you let the white person sit in the

Voice

front, he has a false sense of superiority (and he then believes he can push you in the back)."[13]

Lewis feared for his life while protesting during the movement. As training for the work of civil disobedience, before the sit-ins, the students practiced, role-playing. They learned passive resistance and methods to protect themselves. The most important lesson was to love and forgive those who would challenge them. Their nonviolent protests would often trigger a violent response from white mobs. Lawson taught his students to look perpetrators in the eyes as they strike you on the cheek.

During the lunch counter sit-ins, John Lewis learned to keep loving the people who denied him service. In summary, John Lewis had been trained to love the people who denied his humanity the most. He protested and was knocked down and beaten. But through each bloody altercation, the white mob was given the opportunity to change and to become better. Dr. King said, "We will meet their capacity to inflict suffering with the capacity to endure suffering. Do what you will to us, but we will wear you down."[14] Because of John Lewis and the students' sacrifice, Nashville holds the distinction of being the first Southern city to allow whites and blacks to eat together.

The work of Lewis and others in the civil rights movement was seen as radical for the times. They challenged established albeit unjust Jim Crow segregation laws based on the mandate from St. Augustine, who stated, "An unjust law is no law at all." During recent challenges to the Voting Rights Act, congressman John Lewis said, "There are forces today that want to take us back. But we're not going back. We've come too far. We're going forward. On voter suppression, your voice matters otherwise they would not be trying to shut you up."[15]

So, the question is if we don't have activists willing to sacrifice like John Lewis today, will we lose our democracy? Do we have enough people willing to engage in nonviolent resistance and civil

13. Porter, dir., *John Lewis*.
14. Porter, dir., *John Lewis*.
15. Porter, dir., *John Lewis*.

disobedience? John Lewis is one of the most courageous people of any generation. He was one of the original freedom riders who traveled on desegregated buses to challenge Jim Crow laws in the Deep South. He took all the beatings, and he had lost the sense of fear and only focused on the work. But public transportation in the South was finally desegregated in part through his social activism. Lewis's life teaches us that there is something to be said about the impatience of young people who do not believe in slow progress. Youth are best at pushing for the urgency of the moment. Lewis was the leader of the Student Nonviolent Coordinating Committee (SNCC), and he spoke at the March on Washington at the age of twenty-one.

"We have all been called to do something. You who are so young must continue to lead."[16] This was older John Lewis's call to action for young Americans to serve and to complete the work on voting rights he started. Lewis was a voice for his times. He challenged the American consciousness. On Bloody Sunday in Selma, Alabama on the Edmund Pettus Bridge, Lewis taught us all a valuable lesson: "Get knocked down, get up. Not just blacks, but everyone willing to die for freedom."[17]

I end this urgent letter to my beloved country by harkening back to the timely words of John Lewis, whose life changed the trajectory of our nation and to whom we all, white and black, owe a debt of gratitude for his service to America. He said, "Some forces in America [are] trying to take us back to another period. But we must not let that happen."[18]

Over my head, I see good trouble in the air; Brother Lewis must be somewhere!

Eternally yours,

The Psalmist

---

16. Porter, dir., *John Lewis*.
17. Porter, dir., *John Lewis*.
18. Morin, "John Lewis."

Voice

Part II. Silence

> How absurd is it,
> Silence?
> When one thinks of
> Silence,
> Veiled in comfort
> Risking nothing,
> Preserving mystery,
> Always.
> Like a secret ever kept,
> Silence
> Lives to see another day.
>
> —The Absurdity of Silence
> By Sharon Kimberly Williams

1. Introduction: Silence and Outrage

> "We will have to repent in this generation not merely for the vitriolic words and actions of the bad people, but the appalling silence of the good people."[19]
>
> —Dr. Martin Luther King Jr., *Letter from Birmingham Jail*

Silence is now and has always been a problem. Deafening silence in the face of injustice sparks our most profound sense of outrage and makes our ability to overcome injustice seem as though it is more than an impossibility. This is where my fury begins: In the hypocrisy of silence when justice is denied.

Let me start by stating that I am outraged by the fact that I must assume the burden of writing on the importance of breaking the silence in the face of injustice after so many other voices throughout history have already stated this case so eloquently and

---

19. King Jr., "Letter from a Birmingham Jail."

profoundly. History teaches us that nothing good can occur until the seal of silence is finally broken. I am outraged that some believe achieving social justice and full equality is an impossibility. Those who believe that the inevitability of human suffering is merely a byproduct of the human condition have simply reasoned with a humanistic, myopic vision and minimal regard for the divine.

To those who stand against the tenets of justice, equality, and breaking down barriers of racial disparities, I assume this task of challenging such a limiting ideology with both honor and fury. The lack of understanding of the divine nature of social justice fuels this endeavor and provides hope for an otherwise bleak future. If one's imagination could conceive of a world without the pursuit of justice, what would that world entail? Would life without justice be worth living? My shock and outrage are for those who shamelessly stand on the opposing side of promoting social justice, social change, and the common good.

One must recognize that in the void of silence, there is an indignation that refuses to acknowledge God in the practical formulations of our earthly equations of justice. My outrage for this refusal promotes the peculiar pairing of silence and voice. Silence bears a necessary witness to the double injuries of grief and abandonment in a declaration of the damage done to the souls of humanity when the privileged keep their silence, leaving the oppressed to pay the price. My outrage today is for those who sealed their fate in history by remaining silent on those critical societal issues that define our modern existence.

Those moments constitute the fodder and the fiber, the very substance of what the souls of humanity are made of. My outrage today is for those who dare to ask, with a straight face, impossible questions to all the families of those sons and daughters who recently died while in police custody. *"Is there such a thing as justice?" "There is no real fairness in life." "This is just the way things are." "Life is not fair."*

Questioning the existence of justice creates an existential crisis between the human and the divine. Yet those who deny the existence of justice also deny God. To separate God from justice is futile as God's primary nature is characterized by justice and mercy. As we strive to be more Godlike, we strive to be more just in our character and lived experiences because God and justice are linked by love and compassion. For those who desire to divide the divine from the characteristic of justice, skepticism establishes a stronghold of silence that is likened to an invisible monster. This monster of silence can be imagined keeping all our societal evils alive and well, and thriving against agents of social progress and social change.

In a biblical sense, silence can be likened to an evil monster roaming about. This is what my outrage serves to accomplish today: To reveal the monster of silence for the evil it is. It is my sincerest hope that good women and men might one day be redeemed through the understanding that silence can no longer be a safe haven that hides the dark injustices of society. My anger culminates in a wave of outrage for those who have already and will continue to conspire with silence.

For Christians in the United States who do not know that the tenets of the Christian faith align with divine notions of justice for the poor and the oppressed, may they find redemption for their silent, complicit behaviors that have harmed our nation's progress on human and civil rights. This is what turns my outrage into sadness: For those who hide in silence as people of faith and claim to serve the same God as the oppressed when they deny justice to those suffering from the rise of anti-black violence, your silence is immoral. For those citizens who kept silent and did not speak up during the protests of 2020 or against the insurrection of 2021, for those silent women and men hidden in plain sight in positions of privilege and power, I offer the following ruminations on silence for your consideration.

2. Silence is a Problem

The problem with silence is what it does to the character of good men and women. The problem with silence is that it makes one complicit. The problem with silence is that it makes one complacent. The problem with silence is that it conveys consent. The problem with silence is that it conceals consequences. The problem with silence is that it offers comfort and aid to the enemy. The problem with silence is that it provides a haven for hatred. The problem with silence is that it delays justice. The problem with silence is that it creates chaos. The problem with silence is that it blinds us to the truth. The problem with silence is that it hinders human progress. The problem with silence is that it allows unjust laws to perpetuate. The problem with silence is that it promotes social stagnation. The problem with silence is that it interferes with democracy. The problem with silence is that it is hard to break once kept. The problem with silence is that once it starts, it persists. The problem with silence is that it speaks so loudly, in deafening proportions. The problem with silence is that it controls and contradicts. The problem with silence is that it isolates and excludes. The problem with silence is that it alters one's perceptions. The problem with silence is that it promotes fear. The problem with silence is that it perpetuates ignorance. The problem with silence is that it separates. But the primary problem with silence is that it *kills*. How long will good people remain silent in the face of injustices?

3. Silence of the Good

It has been fifty-eight years since the Dr. King penned the historical and prophetic "Letter from a Birmingham Jail," where he addressed a group of white moderate faith leaders who disapproved of the civil rights movement protest activities taking place in their communities. Throughout this powerfully persuasive letter, written in a scathing rhetorical style, King expressed his disappointment with the group for their hypocrisy as Christian men of faith working against the movements for justice, equity, and social change. Our understanding of the power of persuasive writing for the advancement of social justice was elevated to the pinnacle with the formation of King's transcendent letter. After King's prophetic offering, the segregated world of Jim Crow would never be the same.

On Good Friday in 1963, King was arrested in Birmingham and began to write his letter of rebuke to his fellow clergy members

Voice

while in jail. More than anything, the "silence of the good" trope written into the letter stands out and has been quoted broadly by others for the powerful ways it demonstrated the evil and danger of silence. As noted, Dr. King wrote, "We will have to repent in this generation not merely for the vitriolic words and actions of the bad people, but the appalling silence of the good people."[20] The danger of silence is that it creates a false paradigm where silence can be understood as a willingness to participate in systems that perpetuate privilege, power, and the pursuit of profit. Silence, in this regard, is processed as a strategic tool that releases one from responsibility.

When encountering injustice face-to-face, one can be crippled by indecision, not knowing whether to get involved or stay quiet. The parable of the good Samaritan provides insight into understanding our role in addressing this type of moral justice. Inaction by bystanders is an unforgivable offense. Being a good Samaritan requires sacrifice and remaining silent is often stigmatized by shame. Looking back, the times we failed to be the good Samaritan are the times when we were often left with guilt and shame.

Darnella Frazier, the teenage bystander who filmed George Floyd's public murder by police, is the epitome of a good Samaritan. Had it not been for this young woman's courageous spirit and bold heroism, the offending officer, Derek Chauvin, would not have been convicted, and justice would not have prevailed for George Floyd, his family, other recent victims of police brutality, and our wounded nation. Human nature tends to lean toward apathy when it comes to getting involved in societal issues. We sometimes silence ourselves to avoid responsibility when someone is in need. But Darnella Frazier was not silent. Although she and the other neighborhood bystanders at the crime scene did not possess the power to prevent officer Chauvin from taking his knee and choking the life out of George Floyd, she did not remain silent. She took out her camera phone, and she did what she could do by standing up for a victim of anti-black violence. She did not back down or hide in cowardice even when the officers taunted her and

---

20. King Jr., "Letter from a Birmingham Jail."

threatened her to stop filming. Frazier exemplifies the qualities of the good Samaritan through and through. She is the perfect example of how Dr. King wanted those good clergymen to break their silence in the face of injustice instead of sheltering in silence and fear. Are we as a society fostering a new generation of good Samaritans like Danielle Frazier?

4. Silence and Evil

"Silence in the face of evil is itself evil: God will not hold us guiltless. Not to speak is to speak. Not to act is to act."[21]

—DIETRICH BONHOEFFER

"The only thing necessary for the triumph of evil is that good men do nothing."[22]

—JOHN F. KENNEDY

What is at the root of evil and injustice? Silence. Theologian Dietrich Bonhoeffer who spoke out in resistance to anti-Semitism and lost his life in the process, once stated, "Silence in the face of evil is evil itself." One might ask, "What is so evil about silence?" What is evil about silence is that silence is often followed by great loss. Loss of freedom. Loss of human rights. Loss of civil rights. Loss of humanity. In this instance, the loss of black lives. Once again, this poignant Bonhoeffer phrase is best exemplified in the historical example of America's original sin, which is racism. To be clear, good American citizens sat in silence and allowed chattel slavery for several centuries without taking any moral responsibility to end its human carnage. America's original sin,[23] from which many other sins are born, is directly connected to the evil at the root

---

21. These words are widely and possibly apocryphally attributed to Bonhoeffer.
22. Kennedy, "Address to Canadian Parliament in 1961."
23. See Wallis, *America's Original Sin*.

of American violence, exploitation for profit, and the American Dream. The sin of silence in this country takes much reflection as justice/silence and good/evil are often juxtaposed against the binaries of wrong/right. One chooses which narrative one wants to define one's life and which narrative America wants to define itself. Does one want to join an American narrative on race that reflects action in the face of injustice or silence?

After the Holocaust, the words "Never again" represent the promise that Jewish citizens pledged to never sit in silence in the face of extreme evil. "Never again" becomes, in this instance, a commitment to oneself and one's countrymen and women to never allow the sin of silence to create the conditions for genocide, exile, and erasure. The taboo nature of breaking the silence on the issue of white (Aryan) supremacy in Nazi Germany is similar to what America experienced, albeit to a far lesser degree. America's original sin reflects that the country's current issue with anti-black racism can be traced back to this country not taking responsibility for the crime of slavery and remaining silent.

In America today, increasingly, we are seeing how white silence equals violence. We here in America must never forget the American origins of anti-black violence and racism in the form of slavery. We must confront those who hide under the covenant of silence as we change the narrative and clarify the fallacies inherent in our national identity. This original sin that separates our country from God suggests America must repent for no other reason than for what George Santayana suggested when he stated, "Those who cannot remember the past are condemned to repeat it."[24] Santayana teaches us how silence about America's history can shape our nation's destiny.

Where does the church stand on this discourse about the evils of racism? In America, when the church is silent on the issue of race, it is sinful. This form of silence goes against the liberating teachings of Jesus and makes a mockery of the democratic principles upon which this nation was founded. This silence is reflected in the bloody roots of racism upon which this nation was built.

24. Santayana, *Life of Reason*, 334–35.

Roots that resurface and cause an uproar. Like the series of police-related incidences of violence that led to the mass protests of 2020. The church has been too silent in response to the black bodies that have recently been killed. The Christian church as an institution has yet to conceive a plan for integrating and moving past its own segregated history to accomplish the work of becoming anti-racist and pursuing racial justice. In the church and society, silent complicity is at the root of the construction of whiteness that has as its primary contention the goal of covering white supremacy and institutional racism with the evil of silence.

5. Silence and Absurdity

There is something transcendent and transformative about the absurd silence of the universe. More than anything, the universe's silence makes a case for justice. A philosophy of silence and justice offers a different interpretation of the silence of God. I begin with the cosmos and the silence of the senses, theories of perception, and representational theories of consciousness to highlight the existential crisis of human existence and why we are here, the theodicy of God, and feelings of abandonment that are understood as the absurdity of the indifference and silence of the universe in moments of injustice.

French philosopher and absurdist theorist Albert Camus has written extensively on the unreasonable silence of the world to express his philosophy on the challenges of pursuing justice. The question of theodicy is apparent in Camus's work as he pokes fun at the fact that our earnest pursuits of knowing the mystery of our world only receive the response of silence from God, which is absolutely absurd in Camus's estimation. Thus, Camus's philosophy recommends that we all embrace the absurdity of the silence of God. I submit that it is more important for humanity to continue to grapple with the questions of theodicy in the pursuit of justice and not to abandon God and the moral principles of working toward a more just society.

Voice

One could argue God's silence gives humanity no assurance about anything related to our existence. Nor does it offer any expectations about the quality of justice and fairness to expect from our human experiences. Camus's central argument for absurdity is founded upon our striving to find meaning in response to God's silence. Camus maintains life has no meaning. Without the understanding that God's goodness will prevail and that the arc of the universe will bend toward justice, Camus's theory of absurdity highlights the conflict between questioning our meaning and purpose in life against the lack of response from God and the universe.

Camus on Justice

> Absolute freedom mocks at justice. Absolute justice denies freedom. To be fruitful, the two ideas must find their limits in each other. No man considers that his condition is free if it is not at the same time just, nor just unless it is free. Freedom, precisely, cannot even be imagined without the power of saying clearly what is just and what is unjust, of claiming all existence in the name of a small part of existence which refuses to die.[25]

This contradiction of silence from God and the universe and uncertainty on the issues of justice as absurdism led Camus to suggest that humanity should simply embrace the absurdity of the human condition. Working from the theoretical, existentialist philosophy of the absurd from Søren Kierkegaard, Camus began to delve deeper into absurdism and the European existential movement with his publication *The Myth of Sisyphus*.

6. Silence, Racial Disparities, Anti-Black Racism, and the Myth of Sisyphus

What is the myth of Sisyphus? Sisyphus, the ancient Greek mythological figure who tricked the gods and averted death, was condemned

---

25. Camus, *Rebel*, 291.

by the gods to a form of hell. Sisyphus was punished by the gods, who cursed Sisyphus with the eternal task of repetitive, futile slave labor that required pushing a giant boulder up a hill only to see it roll down again and then start all over, on and on, into perpetuity.

What does this have to do with the meaning of life and the silence of God on issues of injustice, and why does the narrative of Sisyphus matter for black lives? The narrative of Sisyphus puts one in touch with the paradoxical position of justice. One can liken the fight against anti-black racism to a Sisyphean task. The Sisyphean search for truth and meaning in black life is better known as *the struggle*. The same struggle that was known to my parents as the civil rights movement is known to me, their daughter, as the Black Lives Matter movement. Both movements, along with the Black Power movement, are part of the struggle for equality under the law.

The struggle for civil rights, whether it be through the Black Lives Matter movement or any other movement for racial justice, is a repetitious form of activism for liberation and freedom. Each generation must put in the work. Every generation must do its part to create a more just society. Every generation must take its turn. Still, one's efforts may only deliver a sliver of progress. The struggle to seek racial justice and respond to anti-black racism in America seems repetitive and absurd. The effort to overcome racial disparities, anti-black racism, and repeating the mantra "Black Lives Matter" is exhausting. On the one hand, the Sisyphean task of pursuing justice is mundane, and the outcome yields very few returns. But on the other hand, seeking justice and liberation is a process, not a destination.

For those committed to social justice, the work can be likened to an uphill battle in the name of progress. Each generation of sons and daughters must return and reinstate the same civil rights mandates secured by the previous generations of fathers and mothers. Exhausting? Yes. But necessary. We cannot stop! The struggle must go on. In this scenario, the object we tirelessly push up the hill is anti-black racism and racial disparities. The mountain we can never get fully over is white supremacy—the struggle and the stark awareness of racial disparities in all areas of American life.[26]

Camus is challenging us not to imagine Sisyphus stagnant, not continuing his work but being happy with his task because he is content with his work even though there is suffering in the world. Black people in America can relate to the example of Sisyphus in our daily life experiences. We push that boulder up the hill of supremacy, knowing we will never make it "fully" over the mountain's peak of defeating white supremacy and the boulder will roll back down the hill.[27] But in our work—in our commitment to the struggle—we continue working with a commitment to doing justice.

> *"Everyone has it inside himself, this plague,
> because no one in the world, no one, is immune."*[28]
>
> —ALBERT CAMUS

7. Silence in Camus's "The Plague"

The absurd thing about plagues is that they are silent and deadly. With a superpower of invisibility, disease can take multimillion lives and destroy the human species anytime. At the onset of the COVID-19 pandemic, many returned to Camus's 1947 literary classic *The Plague*. Society desperately turned to this book for answers to the unknown as we all lived with an absurd silence from God in response to why so many deaths from COVID-19 were allowed. The existential crisis of why we are all here if only to be wiped out by a random virus confronted our minds and threatened humanity.

In contrasting modern times to the setting of *The Plague*, the initial epidemic and quarantine in Wuhan, China, can be substituted for Oran, Algeria. The coronavirus substitutes the bubonic plague. Life before, life during, life after the plague.

---

26. Morgan, "Black Life and the Myth of Sisyphus."
27. Morgan, "Black Life and the Myth of Sisyphus."
28. Camus, *Plague*, 253.

Disenchantment, exile, and enchantment can be found in both examples. What is the same in both the fictional narrative by Camus and the real-life version we are experiencing today is the silence of the disease that snuck in and took over followed by silence from God, who offered no answer to the absurd number of lives lost. In both narratives, the disease spread across the globe silently from animals to humans, then from human to human.

In both instances, the citizens and the authorities question the problem with the dead bodies of people being collected. Both experienced the feeling of losing freedom due to quarantines and shutdowns—feelings of disenchantment, exile, enchantment, and isolation from loved ones. Accepting the absurdity of pandemics and the existential crisis of contagion is what we are dealing with in these current times. The absurdity that we can all be taken out instantly lets us know that we all carry an evil plague—which is a reality about the human condition to which none are immune.

In 2020, racial disparities in health care during the season of the COVID-19 pandemic demonstrated again how, like Sisyphus, black Americans roll the boulder of health equity and equal access to quality healthcare up the hill, just to see it roll back down. The coronavirus disproportionately impacted black communities, which had the highest infection rates. As all communities including communities of color wrestled with the crisis of the coronavirus, the unveiling of the health disparities and the countless bodies taken by the disease brought us no closer to hearing from God the answer to the existential question: Why are we here if we are only to suffer and die at the hand of a silent, microscopic monster? Spreading silently and uncovering the hidden world of health disparities in America and across the globe, Camus's narrative speaks to the silence and evil of racial disparities in the medical field. As for the fictitious narrative of *The Plague*, the illness was always there. No one was immune. Plagues and pandemics are inevitable realities, and the only explanation we will receive from God and the universe is silence, so we must cling to hope.

8. Silence and Suffering

Life will always have suffering. Yet, Dostoevsky tries to show in his writing that there is always a path to redemption. One of the themes of Dostoevsky's writing is that humanity loves suffering, which is why suffering will never be fully eliminated. This sets up his primary conflict with the pursuit of justice. According to Dostoevsky, the conditions of life will never change. The type of suffering will change but suffering itself remains. Thus, his writing critiques the pursuit of justice and notes that humans actually enjoy the feeling of superiority over one another.

According to Dostoevsky, people do not want to live in a truly equal society. His work critiques modern liberalism to demonstrate some of the challenges with social progress. For example, in *Crime and Punishment* Dostoevsky wants to show us the importance of knowing our true selves, who we are beneath the monster, and how even an average person can become a criminal.[29] Once one understands what one is capable of, the goal then becomes knowing oneself beyond the beast. This process sets up the road to redemption as Dostoevsky delivers the theme that everyone, no matter what they have done, deserves compassion and the love of God. But in moments of absurd suffering like the dual pandemics of racism and COVID-19, why does God remain silent?

It is not realistic that humankind can live in the religious images of perfection that reflect a just world. So why bother? Why address suffering? Life will always have suffering, but Dostoevsky tried to show in his writing that there is always a path to redemption. Regarding Dostoevsky, Baldwin quotes one of the characters in Dostoevsky's *The Idiot*: "I do not believe in the wagons that bring bread to humanity. The wagons that bring bread to humanity may coldly exclude a considerable amount of humanity from enjoying what has been brought."[30] Baldwin states,

> Dostoevsky's character goes through the world with a spirit of pure thanksgiving and gratitude for the simplest

---

29. Dostoevsky, *Crime and Punishment*.
30. Baldwin, *I Am Not Your Negro*, 93.

Breath | Voice | Fire

pleasures in life. No judgment or condemnation of others. No malicious intent. Able to see everyone equally. This enchanted worldview set him up to be identified as "The Idiot" in this narrative, as modern people take the opposite position on all these matters. The human condition is what it is.[31]

In using this quote, Baldwin makes the point, "Well, you read something that you thought only happened to you, and you discover that it happened 100 years ago to Dostoevsky."[32] Two men from different worlds and different generations, Dostoevsky and Baldwin. Both wrote about human suffering within the context of their respective communities in their times. Both men sought to connect humanity and human suffering with an abiding redemptive arc of God.

9. Silence and Resistance in the Arts

"In times of dread, artists must never choose to remain silent."[33]

—Toni Morrison

When the silence is broken one can give voice and meaning to life. By giving voice through artistic expression our world becomes clearer. As we give way to voice by breaking the silence, we make sense of God's silence. Our art is our highest form of expressing love. Our art represents our inner voice. It represents what is in our hearts. From our suffering, we express our love through the arts. In that creative expression of the arts, we are connected to the love of God. This space of love is where we can hear God's voice through the broken silence and believe that our world can be good and just. Dostoevsky states, "The more you succeed in loving, the more you'll be convinced in the existence of God and the immortality of your

---

31. Baldwin, *I Am Not Your Negro*, 93.
32. Baldwin, *I Am Not Your Negro*, 93.
33. Morrison, "No Place for Self-Pity, No Room for Fear."

soul."[34] Thus, we affirm the existence of God and the immortality of our souls through the material, artistic expressions of love. More specifically, as seen throughout the Psalms, God's voice represents a love of justice through an abiding love for the oppressed.

This biblical context for understanding justice as love in action is based on Micah 6:8, which commands us "to do justice, and to love kindness, and to walk humbly with your God." As the psalmist urges us to seek justice for the oppressed, which includes the poor, widows, orphans, and the stranger/foreigner, and all those who are met with the harsh realities of this unjust world, there are a few things we should know. First, God is a God of justice. By doing the work of justice we are required to break the silence, which can be a costly endeavor for those who already exist on the margins.

As we are commanded to work for justice, this mandate takes on a unique role for the psalmist and those who identify as creative and performing artists. Performing artist and jazz legend Nina Simone profoundly states, "As far as I am concerned, an artist's duty is to reflect the times."[35] Simone was an artist-activist who knew her responsibilities to society. Toni Morrison stated what artists must do in times of societal crisis: "This is precisely the time when artists go to work. There is no time for despair, no place for self-pity, no need for silence, and no room for fear. We speak, we write, we do language. That is how civilizations heal."[36]

Two powerful expressions demonstrate artists using their voices and their public platforms to fight for justice. Just as the psalmist must sing praises to God, those who can must use their artistic platforms to break the silence on injustice and give voice to the oppressed. Through music, poetry, novels, sermons, paintings, spoken word, theatrical productions, dancing, and all other forms of artistic expression, artists can dismantle the evil power structures that exist in silence. With our creative imagination, new possibilities and potentialities can help us imagine alternative

---

34. Dostoevsky, *Brothers Karamazov*, 70.
35. Simone, "Artist's Duty."
36. Morrison, "No Place for Self-Pity, No Room for Fear."

worldviews. With our artistic imagination, strategies of resistance that have the power to challenge the status quo are conceived. With our creative imagination, we mobilize and create social justice movements that can change the world. Thus, our duty today is to engage our artistic imagination during these challenging times of crisis and dread, such as our current circumstance of racial unrest during a global pandemic.

In a 1993 interview with Charlie Rose, Toni Morrison spoke poignantly to the pathological mindset that engineered the exact type of anti-black racist thinking required for Officer Derek Chauvin to murder George Floyd in cold blood. Morrison stated,

> How do you feel? Don't you understand that the people who do this thing, who practice racism, are bereft? There is something about the psyche. It is a corruption and a distortion. It is like it is a profound neurosis that nobody examines for what it is. It feels crazy. It is crazy. And it has just as much of a deleterious effect on White people and equality as it does on Black people.

Morrison continues:

> But then you take it away. I take your race away, and there you are. All strung out. And all you got is your little self, and what is that? What are you without racism? Are you any good? Are you still strong? Still smart? Do you still like yourself? I mean, these are the questions?

Lastly,

> If you can only be tall if I am on my knees, then you have a severe problem. And my feeling is White people have a very, very serious problem. And they should start thinking about what they can do about it. Come to grips with your own fears, your own history, and what you need. What do you need this [racism] for? I said glibly a moment ago, "It feels good." It must, or they would give it up. It is wasteful. It wastes a lot. It is ugly. It hurts. Why are you paying for that?[37]

---

37. Morrison, "Interview With Toni Morrison and Charlie Rose."

Voice

The long-awaited crescendo of the Black Lives Matter protests of 2020 caused many whites to finally break their long silence on police brutality and anti-black racism. The movement for black lives took the world by storm and will go down in history as one of the most significant social protest movements in US history. Half a million people gathered in 550 locations across this country to resist anti-black racism. Millions marched, breaking their silence to proclaim the sacredness of black lives. Oddly, Black Lives Matter is a proclamation already made by God at the moment of creation through the imago Dei. Thus, Black Lives Matter was already a divine proclamation that should never have to be made by humans. Yet the sentiment does need to be voiced because of the existential crisis of blackness previously discussed by Du Bois and others.

In June 2020, blackness and what it means to be black in America took center stage. When the George Floyd execution video circulated the world, for that moment, we were all George Floyd. The world was shaken. Black people from the African Diaspora and beyond shared stories of survival of abuse while in the custody of law enforcement. The Black Lives Matter movement had hit a plateau in our national consciousness. Black voices were finally being heard and good people of all races took to the streets. Everyone shared the attitude that we would no longer live under a regime of silence and fear of a racist nation that kills black people without remorse. We all watched the video. Over and over. And then, we watched it again. Crying, questioning, consoling, we desperately sought answers where there were none.

All the while, God remained silent. World-renowned singers, poets, artists, and preachers all gathered at the funeral with expressions of love and lament about what had happened to the body of a beautiful black man called by his closest family members and friends "Big Floyd," the gentle giant. Just Big Floyd. Left in the gutter to die. Life slowly and silently choked out of him at the hands of law enforcement while the entire world watched silently in perplexed amazement at the absurdity of it all.

At once our rage began to burn as anger turned into fury. And then, the silence was no more.

Breath | Voice | Fire

Original Poems and Poetics on Voice

> "And God said, 'Let there be light,' and there was light.
> And God saw the light, that it was good: and God
> divided the light from the darkness."
>
> —Genesis 1:3–4

Like the dawn of a new day never held ransom by the morning sky,
Time freely gives the awakening of voice, not afraid to break the silence.
From broken silence,
All of creation was spoken into existence.
From silence to voice, our world is made more just.
Voices unafraid to fill the void.

On Silence

Silence is where it all begins. That is evil. Man's inhumanity to man. The "necessary evil" we are taught works for "the greater good." And one day, we all grow and learn the shameful truth—that much of the world's evil is made possible by the silence of good people who do nothing in the face of evil. Silence allows evil to grow and take root in fertile ground reserved for sacred work toward just ends. Silence works in the shadow of its own false intentions by those who will never surrender an inch of power to the masses. Silence has shaped our world into whatever state one believes in residing, forcing us to accept what we know to be unacceptable. Silence complicates us, not-so-innocent bystanders, who will never be forgotten on judgment day. Silence is what makes martyrs roll in graves left cold. For the silence of stories untold, someone's shame is the burden one must bear.

Voice

Voice + Silence

Mystery of voice
Into your darkness
Casts shadows upon
Knowing
To me, you are unknown
But in your void
In the nothingness of
Being
I came boldly
Courageously
With sound
Forms of awe
wonderment
against the fray
of broken edges
Forms of life
In the sonic realm
There is a frequency
That animates life
After breath
The elusive prize
Captured for the cause
With bodily instrument
Of chords and tongues
We chronicle our stories
Giving birth to record,
Our sacred time on earth
and what it has meant
to be human
vulnerable

Breath | Voice | Fire

in this grand experiment of
being human
the great gift of spirit
moves us freely
from breath to voice

Voice

Untitled

I speak in weeping tones.
For I am yet grieved
By all that is now
What we've become
Disconnected
Only hurt and pain
I come today to ask,
"Will there be more George Floyds?"
"Will there be more?"
And I am grieved because the answer is already
Yes.
Have we honored the life of the man known as George Floyd?

Breath | Voice | Fire

Voice & Becoming

We become who we are called to be
If only we dared to use our voice
Powerfully, courageously, boldly, unapologetically,
righteously, poetically, prophetically, unashamedly,
persuasively, progressively, conservatively, truthfully,
profoundly, intimately, lovingly, kindly, forcefully,
respectfully, compassionately, spiritually, politically,
communally, selflessly, piously, critically, intelligently,
faithfully, convincingly, concernedly, intentionally. Who
would you be? Who would you become if you used your
voice creatively and colorfully?
In all these small ways, we all can voice.
Be the voice
We become the voice
In becoming the voice
We become one
With the Spirit of truth

What does it mean to voice?
Be the voice
When we voice, we become the voice
We become more just
With the wisdom of truth

What does it mean to voice?
Be the voice
When we voice
We become a voice
We become the voice

Voice

And in becoming the voice.
We become
We are birthed into the realm
Of our highest self
We become
We become when the matters of injustice are voiced
Out of the safe harbors of silence
We become
When we wrestle with the constraints of time
And the psalmist's cry of, "How long?"
Goes unanswered for too long, God
As the dawn of a new day
With voice, we become all
We become co-creators with God
We become intermediaries between this world and the next
Between good and evil
Between the just and the unjust
Between right and wrong
We become intermediaries for the unvoiced
We become whom we speak for

We become a great tapestry
of all the fragments we ever represented
With our spoken voice
We are who we speak for
We are what we speak to
We are what we speak about
We are what we refuse to speak about

As we use our voice
We become perfected in who we are
What we represent
Who we represent
What matters to us
And what ways our words might change the world.
With our voices, we become change agents
We transcend; we improvise

We speak our world
We become creators of our world

Breath | Voice | Fire

We speak our world
We become perfectors of our world
We speak our world
We become interpreters of our world

Voice is breath made manifest in the earth
Voice is breath calling us to purpose
Voice is breath connecting our internal and external worlds
Voice is breath
Voice is the stated intention of breath
Spoken in the physical realm.

Voice

Untitled

Storm of hatred
Time for healing
These times are marked
Anti-Black violence
Pandemic
Insurrection
White supremacy on the rise

Breath | Voice | Fire

Untitled

Breathless
Voiceless
Where is our fire?
First, catch our breath,
Before you speak
And raise our voice,
Breath feeds fire
so, remember to breathe
Before we can catch our fire!
Voice, find your courage
Voice, lead the way
Voice, create a new
Voice, correct, and rebuke
Voice, tell of the reckoning to come
Voice, break the silence!
Voice, break the silence,
Voice, break the silence,
Connect to your breath, voice!
And speak your power,
Voice, speak your power,
Voice, speak your power,
Voice, speak your power,
Connect to your fire, your essence,
And speak truth to power,
Voice, speak truth to power,
Voice, speak truth to power.
Breath, you are the vehicle of Spirit,
Voice, you are the vehicle of breath,
Fire, you need the oxygen of Breath to show your spirit
BVF, you are characteristics of Spirit.

Voice

Individually, you are strong,
But together, you make one mighty force for justice!
Let you be born in this hour
To speak your voice to these times
To speak humility in these times
To speak altruism in these times
To speak truth in these times
To speak power in these times
To speak healing in these times
To speak righteousness in these times
To speak love in these times
To speak kindness in these times
To speak disruption in these times

Breath | Voice | Fire

Breath, Voice, Fire: A Road map to Revolution

You speak of revolution
And we have no other choice but to listen
Not just hear
You speak of revolution to fight for/against
Voice takes us to those revolutionary spaces we fear
That answer, "Not long"
To the question, "How long?"
No more voter suppression
After 400 years of this American experiment
We are here.
We've been here.
Voice takes us to those revolutionary places
Lest we lose it all
We are here. We've been here.
Our democracy is in shambles, but the priority of the day
Is not making a change in society
Voice shows us those revolutionary faces
Who, in the end, will stand for justice?
We are here. We've been here.
Voice, the spirit of resistance, how long?
We are here. We've been here.
We are here,
We are here
No more silence
Voice = Revolution

Chapter Three

Fire

> *"I say—Where is your fire?*
> *I say—Where is your fire?*
> *You got to find it and pass it on ..."*[1]
>
> —Sonia Sanchez

> *"It is a beautiful thing to be on fire for justice ...*
> *there is no greater joy than inspiring and empowering*
> *others—especially the least of these,*
> *the precious and priceless wretched of the earth!"*[2]
>
> —Cornel West

Part I: A Love Letter to the Black Community

Dear black family:

I beg your pardon, but America is a house on fire, and unfortunately, we are in it! As we learned several generations ago in

---

1. Sanchez, "Catch the Fire."
2. West, *Black Prophetic Fire*, 5.

Breath | Voice | Fire

President Abraham Lincoln's 1858 speech *The House Divided*[3], beloved, we must begin to fight fire with fire at some point. Based on excerpts from Gospel of Matthew, the theme of Lincoln's speech is built upon the biblical principle that reads "a house divided cannot stand" and "every kingdom divided against itself is brought to desolation, and every city or house divided against itself shall not stand."[4] Lincoln's purpose for this speech was to offer words of caution that might diffuse tensions around ending slavery and help the nation avoid the undue burden of going to war with itself.

Know the nation was irreconcilably divided on the issue of ending slavery, Lincoln spoke with care, yet he was concerned with one thing only: The preservation of the American union. First and foremost. Preserving the colonies and territories as one sovereign nation was his sole motivation for this historic speech. Not any fantasized notion of his love for the enslaved African and indigenous peoples charged with tilling the land into perpetuity or any romantic desire to set free the souls of millions of captured men and women who would be enslaved indefinitely. The house was divided and was clearly on fire in 1858. And Lincoln's course of action at that time was to fight fire with fire. In this instance, Lincoln's fire came from a powerful speech intended to change the hearts of both pro-slavery and anti-slavery citizens.

Of course, we know that the Civil War was then inevitable for young America. In 1861 the American house divided itself self-righteously on the battlefield in the name of the Lord to salvage the nation's soul. North split against the South in the name of the Lord. Black against white in the name of the Lord. Confederacy against the Union in the name of the Lord. Democrat against Republican in the name of the Lord. Saint against the sinner in the name of the Lord. Slave against master in the name of the Lord. The individual's rights against the greater good or a necessary evil are all in the name of the Lord. And, although civil war could not be avoided, Lincoln did what he could with his speech to fight the divergent forces on both sides that would have held back this democratic

---

3. Lincoln, "House Divided."
4. Lincoln, "House Divided."

Fire

nation indefinitely. With his speech, Lincoln fought fire with his fire to save the American union.

In doing so, he took the initial steps toward cultivating the framework for our reformed American democracy. He then followed through during the war with the Emancipation Proclamation of 1863, an executive order that freed millions of enslaved Africans. As an article of legislation, the Emancipation Proclamation was the fuel for the fire the abolitionists needed to complete their work of fighting America for the freedom of enslaved people. Following the proclamation, Lincoln began making plans for Reconstruction in the South. He began to advocate for the Thirteenth Amendment, which states that slavery is no longer legal in America, "except as a punishment for a crime." This final wording, "except as a punishment for a crime," becomes the basis for the new Jim Crow in the form of the re-enslavement of black Americans through mass incarceration and the American prison industrial complex. So, if mass incarceration exists and prisons must be filled, were we ever freed, black family? Therefore, we must stay vigilant and remain on fire for the justice of our people.

Why then do we have to fight fire with fire today? According to the Brookings Institute, a 2021 national survey estimated that 46 percent of Americans believed the country was heading towards another civil war.[5] If for no other reason, this is simply because a wildfire of hatred is consuming the American house. A hatred that for too long has been conspicuously hidden in the hearts of people. A wildfire raging so out of control that only the fire of justice can fight its flames on its terms with any hope of winning the battle. This wildfire of hatred has caused America to become a divided nation in every imaginable way—divided on American politics, American culture, American nationalism, American identity, American race relations, tolerance, inclusion, diversity, American immigration, democracy, autocracy, gun control, community

---

5. Gale and West, "Is the US Headed for Another Civil War?"

policing, abortion, the origins of this country, and on who belongs in America and who does not. This current crisis of the American divide began following the political divide that started to seriously plague our nation during the election cycle leading up to the 2016 presidential election. This country has not been the same as a nation, politically speaking, since the 2016 election cycle. Since the onset of Trumpism, America has been more polarized than at any other time in modern US history.

We cannot seem to come to a consensus on the economy, health care, voting rights, gun control, or racial equality, which has left American exceptionalism in question. A recent Pew Research Center study revealed that "race, religion, and ideology now align with partisan identity in ways that they often did not in eras when the two parties were heterogeneous coalitions."[6] According to Carothers and O'Donohue, "a powerful alignment of ideology, race, and religion renders America's divisions unusually encompassing and profound. It is hard to find another example of polarization that comparably fuses all three major types of identity divisions."[7] Trumpism with romanticism and nostalgia for the return to a 1950s America would be the worst thing imaginable for black America.

A return to Jim Crow segregation and second-class citizenship without the protection of the law? No, thank you! Frankly, we want no part of Archie Bunker's America today. Instead, we would prefer to keep the legislative strides we have made and continue onward with more progress. Thus, we must begin to fight conscientiously with our fire and our passion for social justice and change before it is too late.

Writing in the abolitionist tradition of Frederick Douglass and the black radical tradition of Frantz Fanon, Cornel West said in

---

6. Dimock and Wike, "America Is Exceptional."
7. Dimock and Wike, "America Is Exceptional."

2014, "It's a beautiful thing to be on fire for justice."[8] And yes, it is a beautiful thing to be on fire to protect our democratic ideals and the human and civil rights of "the wretched of the earth" or the marginalized masses oppressed in this great land. West was right then, and he is right now. Recently, Jamelle Bouie and Martha Jones wrote, "America itself was forged by the marginalized: How the political struggles waged by black Americans forged US democracy." The transcript reads, "black women pointed the nation toward its best ideals . . . like the founding ideals in the Constitution and the Declaration."[9] In that spirit, I would like to expand the conversation and speak more intimately as a black woman in America about precisely what it means to be on fire for justice.

Being on fire for justice is not just beautiful; it is the most essential thing we must achieve to live a life of purpose—a life worth living. To be on fire for justice is to live with a burning purpose in our hearts that seeks the moral and ethical solution to life's challenges over doing what is convenient or profitable. To be on fire for justice is to live a well-lived life where one's actions directly respond to the struggle against anti-black violence and systemic racism. To be on fire for justice is to live a life where one's will and desire align with the divine tenets of the common good. To be on fire for justice is to live a life where one strives to create a world some say could never exist outside of idealistic fantasies or utopian dreams. To be on fire for justice for the entire course of one's life is to live out one's life in beauty, truth, and altruism.

Reaching the highest moral and ethical ideals is to be on fire for justice. To be on fire for justice is to expand democracy and diversity and to promote the notion of inclusion in the American Dream for all, not just a privileged few. To be on fire for justice is to possess an attitude that says one will not settle for the status quo conditions that subject a group of people to anti-black violence through a lack of progressive legislation. To be on fire for justice is to address this nation's antiquated mandates that do not reflect the policy advances made since Jim Crow segregation and the Civil

8. West, *Black Prophetic Fire*, 5.
9. Jones, "America Was Forged by the Marginalized."

Rights Act of 1964. The Civil Rights Act was landmark legislation designed to end Jim Crow segregation and heal a divided nation for generations to come, by addressing the issues of employment, housing, voter registration, and public assembly. The bill leading up to the Civil Rights Act was first proposed in 1963 by John F. Kennedy, a man who was indeed on fire for justice. But Dr. King's advocacy got the bill through Congress and onto President Lyndon B. Johnson's desk and forced lawmakers to vote on this legislation in 1964, when the bill was finally ratified into law.

Black family, now more than ever, we are on fire for justice. Black women are on fire for justice in the evidence of their community activism and political leadership. Black men are on fire for justice. Like combat soldiers, they are sacrificed and racially profiled. Black slain bodies lay crucified on the front lines of today's social justice movements. Through the Black Lives Matter movement, youth and young adults are on fire for justice as generations of millennials, Generation Y, and Generation Z begin to demand from America a paradigm shift that ends the racially stratified caste system in America.

More than anything, our activism defines what it means for black America to be on fire for justice. To be on fire for justice is to have one's life intricately interconnected to the struggle in such a manner that one's *life is the struggle, and the struggle is one's life*. The will and desire one has toward the pursuit of justice is the actual purpose of life, as the pursuit of justice makes life beautiful. This is how my beloved black community has been blessed despite its struggle with American hypocrisy.

To be on fire for justice is to be fully alive. To be on fire for justice is to be aligned with divine justice. To be on fire for justice can also be understood as a yearning that manifests as the unyielding will to do or act against the injustices of the day without compromise. To be on fire for justice is a moral mandate one has with oneself, like a self-fulfilling contract that defines where we stand on the social issues that impact our communities. Our fire challenges what we are willing to sacrifice. As our sacrifices contribute toward creating a more just society, we learn that our deepest, most idealistic values define us. We are defined by those things we are willing to give our lives to protect. We are defined by our fire and how willing we are to use it.

The black community has survived by responding to white supremacy and anti-black violence with nonviolent campaigns of civil disobedience and Black Power Movement campaigns of "by any means necessary." Some believe the love and compassion that undergirded Dr. King's method of a slow and steady civil disobedience campaign, with nonviolent tactics in the face of water hoses and billy clubs, made a substantive difference toward long-term racial reforms in America. We should begin to take to heart the mandate to black America inherited from James Baldwin in "The Fire Next Time," which teaches us that we must love as a duty those who hate us most, or there is no hope for this democratic nation or the people who reside in it.[10] Without love, there would be no hope for this American experiment.[11] Baldwin speaks to this concept best when he writes to his nephew about black Americans' duty to love their white brothers and sisters.

> Please try to be clear, dear James, through the storm that rages about your youthful head today, the reality behind the words acceptance and integration. There is no reason for you to try to become like White people, and there is no basis for their impertinent assumption that they must accept you. The terrible thing, old buddy, is that you must accept them. And I mean that very seriously. You must accept them and accept them with love. These innocent people have no other hope. They are, in effect, still trapped in a history that they do not understand; and until they understand it, they cannot be released from it. They have had to believe for many years, and for innumerable reasons, that black men are inferior to White men. Many of them, indeed, know better, but, as you will discover, people find it very difficult to act on what they know. To act is to be committed, and to be committed is to be in danger. In this case, the danger, in the minds of most White Americans, is the loss of their

---

10. Baldwin, "My Dungeon Shook," 20–21.
11. Baldwin, "My Dungeon Shook," 20–21.

identity. Try to imagine how you would feel if you woke up one morning to find the sun shining and all the stars aflame. You would be frightened because it is out of the order of nature. Any upheaval in the universe is terrifying because it so profoundly attacks one sense of one's own reality. Well, the black man has functioned in the White man's world as a fixed star, as an immovable pillar, and as he moves out of his place, heaven, and earth are shaken to their foundation. You have, and many of us have, defeated this intention; and, by terrible law, a terrible paradox, those innocents who believe that your imprisonment made them safe are losing grasp of reality. But these men are your brothers—your lost, younger brothers. And if the word integration means anything, this is what it means: that we, with love shall force our brothers to see themselves as they are, to cease fleeing from reality and begin to change it. For this is your home, my friend. Do not be driven from it; great men have done great things here, and will again, and we can make America what America must become...You know, and I know, that the country is celebrating one hundred years of freedom one hundred years too soon. *We cannot be free until they are free.*[12]

According to Baldwin, love is the answer to racism in America and we must love our white brothers and sisters as our freedom depends on it. Can solving America's race issue be that simple? Perhaps. Still, the reality is that more radical tactics of the black Power movement were also necessary for our development as an authentic democratic nation. But in the end, black America, we must love our brothers and sisters who hate us. Those who continue to punish and marginalize our masses through racist policies of segregated housing, education, health care, employment, biased policing, and the American judicial systems. With all the racial atrocities we have endured in this country, we are still expected to love our brothers and sisters who do not see us as full citizens who can be partakers of the American Dream. Why? Because, according to Dr. King, Jesus, and James Baldwin, there is no other way.

12. Baldwin, "My Dungeon Shook," 20–21.

Fire

For it is in the depths of compassion and the excellent form of loving and loving and loving and loving your enemy that melts their hardened heart once and for all. As much as we see the need to be on fire for justice as a means of survival for black communities, we must never discount or underestimate the power of Jesus' mandate to love thy brother as thyself. Unconditionally.

As a black woman in America, I am on fire for justice. I serve her when I say her name. Justice. The mysterious, elusive one that often escapes our sense of reason. While American democracy selfishly demands of me a particular and peculiar sacrifice in her name, resistance forces me to blaze my unique path in service to my community. The myth of the strong black woman never allows me to fully rest in America. The strong black woman's tale demands much more from me than I can give. As my soul often collapses under the weight of the burden, I recognize that I do not have to be the general manager of all things in America. Yet our history as black women in America is complicated.

Yes, we are on fire for justice and carry the thankless banner for safeguarding American democracy, which entails endless responsibilities. This should not be taken as a complaint. But respectfully, we would just like to retire from this position in American society. Not to have to be a mammy or a Jezebel. Being a strong black woman places an albatross of unrealistic stereotypes on us, with the expectation that we must always be a Superwoman. We were never allowed to be weak. America demands that we constantly project strength as if we are invulnerable. Invulnerable to pain and fear and hurt and death. Despite this tragic misunderstanding of who we are, for those of us who are on fire for justice, we will keep the flame of justice alive. Although service to her often comes at a tremendous cost to our mental and physical health, I am humbled and honored to be a part of the diverse coalition fighting for justice during these uncertain times. We are not immune to American violence. But the work continues . . .

Breath | Voice | Fire

My life has always centered around the two themes: *Justice* and *Spirit*. The pursuit of knowing justice and understanding her ways has guided every aspect of my life. From settling playground offenses as a child in my small-town neighborhood of Mount Vernon, New York, to refereeing family conflicts and disputes in my home as an adolescent, I am and will always be known as "the peacemaker." It is plain and straightforward who I am—a maker and maintainer of peace. In 2015, my love of justice led me to religious studies and theological education at Drew University Theological School. I am forever changed by the successful season of theological exploration that formally introduced me to the academic study of justice through my primary research areas of the Bible, culture, religion, and society.

Theological education has shaped who I am today. My self-identity is based on a value system that prioritizes justice, compassion, peace, altruism, community, and the common good. It has taken me a long time to grasp what it means to commit one's life spiritually, mentally, and physically to these higher moral and ethical values ascribed to social justice activism and to understand the cost of the commitment. I recognize the heavy burden working for justice can put on one's life. Yet, with my Christian faith as a foundation, I have accepted this justice calling on my life, and I am willing to do the work that is required of me to become a more effective change agent in these unique times. My responsibility to myself requires me to continue in the legacy of social justice as due diligence to support the work I am called to do. This higher calling to justice motivates me to continue studying, researching, and working toward social change as a health advocacy activist, performing artist, and educator.

I understand that the work of justice is a ministry call on my life, and I bear witness to the late Dr. King, who gave his life in the pursuit of justice. His life itself was a ministry and the embodiment of justice and spirituality. My love of justice and Spirit has taught me the importance of reaching my fullest potential as an artist, activist, and scholar. The same pursuit of justice and Spirit will drive me to continue the work for the length of my days.

As an artist-activist with over two decades of experience touring abroad, I have served as a global ambassador for the cultural and performing arts. I have traveled worldwide to more than twenty-five countries performing various forms of black sacred music, including the spirituals, gospel, hymns, Psalms, and poetry. Through my research with the Religion and Global Health Forum on black sacred music, culture, healing, and the arts, my work advocates for eliminating health disparities for marginalized communities worldwide. During this critical time when we are fighting for our democratic values, I am passionate about the unique role black sacred music plays in culture and in promoting our communities' health and healing.

Black family, the ancestral souls cry out to you. Do you hear? Can you hear me? Still, I feel in my heart that there is more that God requires of me. It is like a deep yearning that compels me to do so much more. To be so much more. To love so much more. To be fully present in the moment so that I might be able to respond accordingly to my community. To be more connected to the struggle and more available for action and activism when necessary. To be present when the community is in crisis. Not just to continue to ask questions about getting involved but to knock down doors and leap over boundaries.

To stop at nothing until I identify more ways I can work in the struggle. To show up. To go to the scene. To act. To do something. To lament. To weep and wail. To pray. To sing. To dance. To be fearless. To march. To protest. To resist. To scream. To be silent. To write. To bring my fire. To get my beautiful fire. Always. To live on fire for justice. That is how we keep the house from burning down with us in it. When we fight fire with our fire, it's a beautiful thing. We must be on fire for justice to make any actual change in this world. It is beautiful to be on fire for justice, but we must also learn to "catch the Fire . . . and pass it on."

Breath | Voice | Fire

1. "Catch the Fire": A Tribute to Sonia Sanchez

Black family, "Where is your fire?"[13] I say, "Where is your beautiful fire?"[14]

In 1995, renowned poet Sonia Sanchez posed this question as she paid homage to our foremothers and forefathers of the Middle Passage and the civil rights movement. She paid tribute to our ancestors who fought Jim Crow segregation with their fire. We fought slave catchers and overseers. We were on fire for justice. It was a beautiful thing. We fought the Klu Klux Klan with our fire. We were on fire for justice. It was a beautiful thing. We fought racist sheriff's departments and police brutality in the Deep South with our fire. We were on fire for justice. It was a beautiful thing. We fought segregationist lawmakers for the Civil Rights Act of 1964. And won! We were on fire for justice. It was a beautiful thing. We fought caste systems of Apartheid at home and abroad. We were on fire for justice, and it was a beautiful thing.

Whether with the civil rights movement and civil disobedience or Black Power and the black radical tradition, the black family knows how to fight and survive in America. The black family knows when to fight. We know how to fight in city hall and congressional halls. We know how to fight our way out of ghettos and into covenanted communities. We know how to fight contradictions in the Constitution and discrepancies in the Declaration of Independence. We know how to fight white lies. Lies that are burning the house down. As the forgotten stepchildren of the nation, we have learned to fight America with the best tool imaginable: American hypocrisy. With this mirror, we show America its self-reflection to know who it truly is. We have learned to fight America, a house on fire, with our fire, the love of justice.

With our fire for justice born out of the oppression we endured. Our demand for this country to live out the sacred content of its creed before God is what made America great in the first place. Now American democracy is on fire, and we must fight this

---

13. Sanchez, "Catch the Fire."
14. Sanchez, "Catch the Fire."

fire, fueled by white lies and fantasies, with our beautiful fire of justice for the survival of the beloved community. Our beautiful fire demands of this nation equal humanity of all citizens in the form of equal social, political, and economic status for all its brothers and sisters. Our beautiful fire demands equal representation under the law and that antiquated segregationist laws be removed from the local, state, and national judicial systems. We fight America, a house on fire, with the fire of the love of a people who have a personal stake in saving those democratic ideals that have the potential to save black Americans from destruction, genocide, and erasure.

We must fight with our beautiful fire to save American democracy, using everything we have, including the fire passed on to us by our ancestors. We must gain the courage to accept the gift of ancestral fire. Our very lives depend on it.

I say, *Where is your beautiful fire?*[15] Apocalyptic fire with the power passed down within the black family from generation to generation. Fire is being passed down as a tool. From the heat of their anger because of enslavement and colonialism, the African ancestors passed on their black fire to our modern generations for survival. As the poet Sonia Sanchez has written, the fire has been passed down "from Nat Turner and Garvey and DuBois and Fannie Lou Hamer and Martin and Malcolm and Mandela."[16] We see black fire today everywhere. Like little fires setting this world ablaze, the people of the African Diaspora dispersed us around the globe to lead humanity to the pathway to justice.

We see black fire everywhere we look in culture. We see the prophetic fire of the Black Church on full display, leading the response to racial equity and crimes against individual members of the black community. Like Shadrach, Meshach, and Abednego, we have gone through the fire on these American shores. Beautifully. We have been singing in the fire with our spirituals since we landed on the American shores of Virginia in 1619. We sing our song in the

---

15. Sanchez, "Catch the Fire."
16. Sanchez, "Catch the Fire."

fire to, in the words of Sonia Sanchez, "Be the Fire"[17] that American democracy demands of us. Sonia Sanchez teaches us through her poem that the sacred fire passed on from the ancestors has helped black Americans survive in this strange land. To this day, ancestral fire is intertwined into the very fabric of black American culture.

Look closely. The sparks are there. Black fire can be seen through the interpretive performing arts. Black fire appears in modern manifestations of rap music, Black Girl Magic, Afrofuturism, Black Panthers and its fierce tribe of Wakandan female warriors. Our duty to the ancestors is to do what Sonia Sanchez has requested as a sacred call to action for the black community: Catch our fire or our genius for survival. Dig deep inside ourselves. Find it, and do not be afraid to fight fire with fire. It's a beautiful thing, your fire. America is depending on your fire! Catch it and pass it on.

Eternally yours,

The Psalmist

Part II: Embodied Fire

1. Bones

> *"Oh Lord, you have enticed me, and I was enticed; you have overpowered me, and you have prevailed. I have become a laughingstock all day long; everyone mocks me. For whenever I speak, I must cry out, I must shout, "Violence and destruction!" for the word of the Lord has become for me a reproach and derision all day long. If I say, 'I will not mention him, or speak anymore in his name,' then within me, there is something like a burning fire shut up in my bones; I am weary with holding it in, and I cannot."*
>
> —JEREMIAH 20:7–9

---

17. Sanchez, "Catch the Fire."

Fire

What happens to a prophet when he is finally able to denounce his persecutors? How does the body interpret that inescapable burning sensation within him? In the case of the prophet Jeremiah, who was caught prophesying in Topheth, a city located near Jerusalem in the Valley of Hinnom (Gehenna), where the Lord had sent him, his experience is understood as the divine words of justice having the sensation of an internal fire trapped or locked up inside his bones. Because what needed to be said was so powerful and essential, these prophetic words of rebuke or reckoning that were given to Jeremiah by God created an embodied experience causing the innermost aspect of the individual's body to feel as if it was on fire, burning from the inside out.

Topheth, a place known for ritual fire, burning, and burnt offerings involving children, was an ancient city. Jeremiah was sent to deliver prophetic words of God's judgment coming upon them for their unsanctioned sacrifices worshipping false gods. Jeremiah spoke the Lord's prophetic words to the people of Topheth, which promised disaster so great that they would soon become known as a "valley of slaughter," promising to make their land a "city of horror." For Jeremiah, prophetic words of justice come from the divine to assist humanity in solving societal conflicts that cannot be easily resolved.

The Lord speaks to Jeremiah and says, "Is not my word like fire, says the Lord, and a hammer that breaks rocks in pieces?" Rocks represent the obstacles in our society that no matter what we do or how hard we try, we cannot make our way through the stones that are blocking our paths and keeping us from going forward. Thus it follows that the prophetic fire of the word of God characterized by justice is deposited in the bones of the prophet. Bones in human form contain the fire of the prophetic word of God until it is time for the word to be voiced. The fire in the bones of the prophet manifests as voice. Fire is the essence of a prophetic voice that breaks through our lives' rocks and hard places. This combination of voice and fire understands the connection between prophetic fire and prophetic voice. Because that fire burns within the very bones of a person, it cannot be contained indefinitely.

Breath | Voice | Fire

It must manifest itself as a voice for justice to be made manifest on earth. In the case of the prophet, trying to hold God's prophetic word in his body made him weary. The Scripture says he could not keep in God's prophetic word to Topheth for exceptionally long. Because God's words of justice come to our earthly bodies in the form of prophetic fire, they are intended to be spoken as a prophetic voice. When God gives a prophetic word, it must go forth to the people.

More than any other literary figure, James Baldwin understood this dilemma presented in the biblical interpretation of Jeremiah. In his 1965 essay "The American Dream and the American Negro," Baldwin laments, "I find myself, not for the first time, in the position of a kind of Jeremiah."[18] The fire shut up in the bones of James Baldwin had to do with the words of fire he prophesied about an eloquent literary style and fierce imagination against racialized subjugation in America. Baldwin's fire was about critiquing the Western system of reality. A system of governance argues in European fashion whether it is moral or ethical for one civilization to subjugate, colonize, enslave, or erase other civilizations.

Like the prophet Jeremiah, Baldwin found himself speaking prophetically to the people of his generation about their moral and ethical failures as they relate to black Americans' narrative in this nation. Baldwin's work critiques the notion of the American Dream against the existential crisis of black identity and finding one's place in the world.

In this essay, Baldwin states,

> It is a terrible thing for an entire people to surrender to the notion that one-ninth of its population is beneath them. Until the moment comes when we, the Americans, are able to accept the fact that my ancestors are both black and white, that on that continent we are trying to forge a new identity, that we need each other, that I am not a ward of America, I am not an object of missionary charity; I am one of the people who built the country—until this moment comes there is scarcely any hope for

---

18. Baldwin, "American Dream and the American Negro."

Fire

the American Dream. If the people are denied participation in it by their very presence, they will wreck it. And if that happens, it is a very grave moment for the West.[19]

Like the prophet Jeremiah, Baldwin offers a harsh rebuke to those who celebrate the Western system of government under American Jim Crow, which allows the identity of black people to be relegated to second-class citizenship without any discussion of reform. In the famous James Baldwin-William Buckley debate at the University of Cambridge, Baldwin goes further on his point about the black existential crisis: "The American Dream is at the expense of the American Negro."[20] This is somehow still relevant today. In this debate, again, Baldwin likens himself to the prophet Jeremiah, and much of the content in the discussion is like the essay previously mentioned. The difference in these two presentations of Baldwin's ideologies is the fact that in the debate, Baldwin makes the case that American prosperity and its extension of the American promise has come at the expense of strategically and systematically denying the black segment of this nation's population full access to the American Dream and all that it entails.

"I am one of the people who built the country—until this moment; there is scarcely any hope for the American Dream because the people who are denied participation in it by their presence will wreck it. If that happens, it is a very grave moment for the West."[21] As Baldwin outlines the ways black Americans have contributed to the development of this country, he states, "I picked cotton, and I carried it to the market, and I built the railroads under someone else's whip for nothing."[22] Those who deem themselves true Americans in this land do not understand what it means to work toward building a nation without getting anything in return. To work and build wealth for others while mired in poverty.

This more explicit version of Baldwin's language shows the existential crisis inherent in the flawed American Dream. If we are

19. Baldwin, "American Dream and the American Negro."
20. Baldwin, "Baldwin-Buckley Debate."
21. Baldwin, "Baldwin-Buckley Debate."
22. Baldwin, "Baldwin-Buckley Debate."

all to be truly equal, the dream is essentially "wrecked." A flawed ideology that reasons illogically why am I a good American citizen, working so hard if I am just going to be "equal" at the end of the day? Human nature tells us how people want to be better than the "other," not equal to the "other." Baldwin found this kind of paradox like fire shut up in his bones as he issued the call for racial justice. Baldwin's fire was necessary then and now. His framing of how this nation lacks racial equity in the presence of a democratic government structure is the best social analysis thus far. Baldwin fought on the front lines to help us understand the problem's depths. James Baldwin will always be our literary prophet, our eloquent Jeremiah. As with the prophet, the fire of divine justice was shut up in his bones until the day that he died—still teaching us how to connect prophetic fire with our prophetic voice until the very end.

2. Tongues

"And when the day of Pentecost was fully come, they were all with one accord in one place. And suddenly, there came a sound from heaven like a mighty rushing wind, filling all the houses where they were sitting. And there appeared unto them cloven tongues like as of fire, and it sat upon each of them. And they were all filled with the Holy Ghost and began to speak with other tongues, as the Spirit gave them utterance."

—ACTS 2:1–4

I have always been fascinated by the spiritual phenomenon of speaking in tongues. As evidence of the indwelling of the Holy Spirit in human vessels, this mysterious language has been a source of edification for faith believers since the day of Pentecost. As a witness, I can attest to the pure rapture of the experience. It has always been the most enthralling sacred act. As a woman of faith growing up in the black church who also performed gospel music, speaking in tongues is part of my cultural heritage. This is a gift that I have experienced personally. I often wondered why God made this particular gift in the first place. When I was a

Fire

small child growing up in the seventies, my family and I attended Grace Baptist Church, a dignified Baptist church in my small town of Mount Vernon, New York. Everything about this church was dignified. Exemplary. Regal. Upscale. This church and its pastor, Dr. Franklyn Richardson, were considered black church royalty. Every Sunday during worship service, the church celebrated the Christian faith in its pageantry. Big hats, sharp suits, and flowers in lapels. The works! All done to offer one's best to God in the utmost dignified fashion. What a glorious sight for my little eyes to behold.

I always felt safe in that space. Protected. Secure. With quiet grace, I sat and watched so many things I had no idea would shape my world and the woman I would become. Each week, Reverend Richardson would sing in the most beautiful baritone voice, "There is room at the cross for you . . . You may be high, you may be low, some are rich, some are poor, But there is room at the cross for you." And hearing that, I knew that I would survive my circumstances and the racially subjugated location where I found myself in the world. I understood this at an early age. My mother took my sisters and me to church every Sunday without fail. The Lord's day was the Lord's day, and that is all there was to it. Sunday service was the centerpiece of our lives that every other thing would build upon, which is strange because my father never attended church. He did not believe in going. Did not trust or like preachers. So, for the rest of the family, we continued the tradition without him. Still, it was peculiar to be there without him in this place that was shaping my young world. All the people speaking over me and influencing my life.

By the time I was twelve years old, I had begun visiting the church of one of my friends from my local middle school. This church was Little Friendship Unified Freewill Baptist Church, led by Bishop C. N. Edwers. Because this was another Baptist church, my adolescent thinking was that the worship experience would be like what I experienced at Grace. Calm. Subdued. Somber. And most of all, dignified! But the Unified Free Will congregation only a few blocks away was much more expressive in their worship and liturgical style. Later in my adult life, I learned that this style of Baptist church worship had an unofficial name. Bapticostal.

Bapticostal is a colloquial term that denotes a hybrid of two church worship experiences: The Baptist and the Pentecostal. And it was lively. The more I witnessed through my twelve-year-old eyes these moves of the Spirit and free worship styles, the more fascinated I became. This church had dignified members and a tone of respectability but to a lesser degree than Grace. Little Friendship had members who shouted and danced and ran around the church under the influence of the Holy Spirit. But best of all, people spoke in tongues. And wow! Just like that, I got baptized, changed my church membership, and my mother came with me to the new church.

I had never witnessed anything so otherworldly. Here at this church, Little Friendship, is where I first cultivated my love of justice and Spirit. This space set the foundation for me to "catch and learn and be the fire" during my formative years, thus setting the tone for the fire of activism and scholarship on justice I would work on professionally as an adult.

Does glossolalia or speaking in tongues empower communities to challenge socioeconomic injustices? In *Thinking in Tongues: Pentecostal Contributions to Christian Philosophy*, James K. A. Smith states that "at least on a certain level or from a certain angle, tongue speech could be seen as the language of the dispossessed—or the language of the multitude."[23] In this way, the mysterious ancient tongues have an inherent mode of resistance that automatically challenges unjust worldly systems. In tongues speech, the language speaks truth to power and empire from a moral and ethical divine positioning as God's justice supersedes humanity's earthly justice. As the language of the multitude, Smith characterizes tongues as subversive, counterculture language that is more befitting of those experiencing exile.

---

23. Smith, *Thinking in Tongues*, 148–49.

Fire

This Pentecostal worldview Smith writes about is grounded in social justice principles that highlight a "preferential option for the marginalized,"[24] which historically links to the biblical narrative of the fishermen who were present at Pentecost. This ideology of empowering the marginalized permeates all aspects of the Pentecostal mission and ministry and speaks to the notion of being on fire for justice. Smith writes of the first principle of Pentecostalism and describes it as "the revolutionary activity of the Spirit always disrupts and subverts the status quo of the powerful."[25] This counterintuitive notion of the weak overpowering the strong exemplifies the power of God working through the Spirit. Tongues speech, in this context, is a divine gift intended to transform our modern society in the image of God's kingdom. "Pentecostal spirituality translates into a social program that seeks to embody the kingdom amid a broken creation—a Pentecostal rendition of the social gospel."[26]

If tongues could speak, what would they say about you, America? Would they say the game is rigged? That the entire system marginalizes the Other? That the whole premise for American democracy was predicated on a lie? Would they have the language to articulate in native tongues the fact that you are burning? Or would they need to get a language interpreter to translate your words because you are being misunderstood? If tongues could speak, would they pronounce for your virtues or against your vices? Or would they speak for your vices and against your virtues? Would they defend your evils? Or would they blaze prophetic fire across your land, burning every trace of your hypocrisy? If tongues could speak, would they speak of love for this country or hatred? If tongues could speak, would they speak of surrender or revolution? If tongues could speak, would they speak of justice for the oppressed or maintaining the status quo for the powerful? If tongues could

24. Smith, *Thinking in Tongues*, 45.
25. Smith, *Thinking in Tongues*, 45.
26. Smith, *Thinking in Tongues*, 45.

speak, would they finally speak of decentering whiteness and racial equality? If only tongues could speak, would they speak like fire? Tongues of fire and brimstone holding the church to account. Tongues of prophetic fire that shape our world in God's economy of justice. Tongues of eternal fire with the moral conviction speak of rebuke and the wages of sin. If only tongues could speak the truth. If only . . .

Part III: Backfire

Remember when Los Angeles was burning in 1992? Remember when Chicago was burning in 1919? Remember when Baltimore was burning in 1968? Remember when Newark was burning in 1967? Remember when Watts was burning in 1965? Remember when Detroit was burning in 1967? Remember when Philadelphia was burning in 1918? Remember when Tulsa was burning in 1921? Remember when Rosewood was burning in 1923? Remember when New York was burning in 1900? Remember when Ferguson was burning in 2014? Remember when Atlanta was burning in 2020?

I will be the first to admit boldly that sometimes we burn it down. Not always, but sometimes. Yes, we burned down American tyranny and hypocrisy in the form of American cities set aflame by its forgotten sons and daughters. Sometimes white supremacy burned us down. As in Tulsa. But sometimes, we burned ourselves to the ground in a contradictory spectacle of grand splendor and majesty. Why would anyone burn down their communities, one may ask? This type of pyromania might seem pathological even.

Well, often, something awful has happened, and life no longer makes sense. So, the community responds with destruction in the form of fire. The absurdity of burning down possibilities without even a second thought to human safety or the sanctity of life. It is maddening and inconceivable even to attempt to rationalize irrational actions such as these acts of ultimate despair. But do these reasons for burning down communities have *any* pride? They do. As we examine the historical record of race riots in this nation, are we to believe that black Americans just torched their communities

Fire

in what could be perceived as seemingly reactionary ways without merit or just cause for such revolutionary actions? Is it that we burned down significant cities based on victimizing ideologies or moral principles merely to get the world's attention?

Nothing captures one's attention so completely as fire does. Beautiful fire for all the world to see and know our struggle in America, right? Not necessarily in this instance. With a single stroke of a matchstick, did we torch our hope for a better tomorrow to satisfy an uncontrollable emotional response to communal trauma? Did we ignite potentiality and promise because of pessimism about current socioeconomic and political circumstances? Where is the bold imagination for Afrofuturism or visions of what a genuinely democratic America can be actualized? Did those flames of resistance accomplish anything in a nation so unwilling or unable to honestly face the tides of change crashing against its solemn shores? One might ponder these questions and so many more. Under the ever-lurking gaze of whiteness that gives nothing, not even one inch of power, without a struggle, one may ask if our fiery protests have simply backfired.

The year 2022 marked the thirtieth anniversary of the LA Riots that followed the acquittal of the four officers who were filmed beating an unarmed black man named Rodney King. I was an undergraduate student studying at Howard University when these events took place. The American media descended on Howard's high-profile campus in hopes of catching a polarizing reaction to the verdict from the students and faculty. Some of our Howard professors were ex-members of the black Panther Party for Social Change or civil rights leaders. Many Howard students were the sons and daughters of renowned civil rights leaders or Black Power movement activists. Howard's legacy as "the mecca" for black America still stands today. The black community has always cherished Howard, so whenever something big happens in American culture, Howard is one of the places to go for social commentary and critical analysis.

In the months following the verdict, our entire student body was focused on the King trial at every step. Our professors held student forums allowing us to vent or express our feelings and to unpack the various scenarios that might occur involving the jury's decision to render a non-favorable verdict. Our Howard professors knew something about the American social contract with black folks that we twentysomethings did not know. Our teachers, as our elders in our campus community, knew that right or wrong, America had done too much to establish itself as a law-and-order nation to now radically change its policies on community policing by arresting police officers.

The action of setting any new precedents that altered the current policies toward community policing, over-policing, or the use of excessive force would have a devastating effect on the national psyche. In other words, Americans love the notion that the police are here for their safety, first and foremost. Nothing can change that image, so the men and women in blue have carte blanche and can do whatever they want while engaged in community policing. The officers who beat Rodney King were acquitted a year after the incident. And it was that verdict that ignited the fires that burned in LA.

But this expression of fire was nothing new in 1992. We have seen this repeatedly throughout American history and will surely see it again. A long history of destroying black neighborhoods always occurs after incidents categorized as police brutality, over-policing, and policing with excessive force. How does this happen? Officers show up in black communities to respond to legitimate incidents and may end up looking for other criminal activity where none exists. How else does this abuse occur? Police unload their firearms without sufficient provocation. Dispatch helicopter units or call in the National Guard when deemed necessary. Escalating minor infractions (e.g., selling loose cigarettes—Eric Garner; or passing a counterfeit bill—George Floyd) that escalate into instantaneous death sentences. Howard University students responded

Fire

to King's verdict by marching in a peaceful protest from the Justice Department to the White House.

Most of our nation's outrage around the verdict in the King case had to do with the fact that for the first time as a nation, we all watched the video of the unarmed black man being beaten mercilessly by the police together on television. And once the disappointing verdict was handed down and all four officers were set free, the fires started—one by one. And the LA community began to burn from the inside. It was burning from the inside because that was where the community trauma was. That's where the pain was, on the inside. And that pain was real, palpable. That pain and those raw emotions following the finality of the "not guilty" verdict had nowhere else to go. That pain had no other way to manifest itself. The pain was trapped on the inside. It had no other way to be seen. Once the judge said, "not guilty," the pain had nowhere else to hide. So, the community's pain ignited and burst into flames. And that is how LA was set on fire.

What is a fire in this context? Fire is a representation of the community's anger about injustices leveled against them. Fire represents the fed-up community saying to an apathetic nation, "Can you see the pain you are causing?" Fire represents the community saying, "Since you can't see the pain that you are causing—let us help you see us and understand how your actions are destroying us." Fire represents a rebuke and the warning of reckoning to get your house in order before it is too late. Fire is a representation of breaking down or deconstructing that which cannot be easily fixed so that one can reconstruct or build it up again, but better.

Based on this nation's history of race riots in response to gun violence, police shootings, and over-policing, one can safely ascertain that America is on fire. Democracy is on fire; if the house burns down, just remember that you are in it. How do we know this? Where is the proof of this? Because our communities are on fire. Everywhere. Fires are burning from the north to the south and the east and the west. Fires are trying to find their voice. Fires trying to speak so they can warn us before it is too late. "Listen! The house is on fire!"

Breath | Voice | Fire

America's on fire from the white supremacy that burns in the hearts of people. Everywhere. Like the fire of hatred and anti-black violence. How do we know for sure that America is on fire? Because our communities are burning, and we set the fires ourselves. Like fires burning everywhere at once, America's hypocrisy on the issue of race has been slowly and continually burning down the house for hundreds of years. These fires are just a warning about the dangers of white supremacy and how fires burning everywhere make for a dangerous situation in America. While going through these fires, America must focus and find the courage to stand against white supremacy and white nationalism.

Why is fire being used as a methodology for change? Can the fires set from within the house be about scorching everything and starting over? Perhaps. Author Celeste Ng's symbolism of little fires in response to her traveling metaphor on blinding whiteness says it best when she writes: "The earth, everything was black. Scorched. It felt exactly how I felt. It felt like the end of the world . . . Sometimes you have to scorch everything to start over. The soil is rich. Life can grow there. It's even better than it was before. People are like that as well. Resilient. Even from total devastation, they start over. They find a way."[27]

My beloved black family, we have survived living in a society that demands from us that which it cannot give—love, compassion, empathy. Therefore, when we speak of violence or retaliate with violence in any form, even when justified, our statements or actions are often turned back upon us, our justice-seeking efforts are negated, and we lose the advantage of having the high moral ground, which is needed to win the long game of gaining racial equity (i.e., the civil rights movement). For their defense, our detractors will say about us, "We sold our people into slavery." Or "They burn down our communities." And "Have you seen the latest statistics for black-on-black crime?"

---

27. Ng, *Little Fires Everywhere*, 295.

Fire

These scapegoats lend credence to the deplorable treatment black Americans receive in this country and justify America's long legacy of anti-black racism. With all of this in mind, still, we cannot solely blame white supremacy for the horrific conditions that many of our people find themselves in today. As a community, we must look into ourselves and look to our ancestors for the fire that sustains us, not America or America's systems. The answers to our predicament in America and throughout the African Diaspora lie in our ancestral fire. Therefore, part of our work is that we must find our fire to protect our own from destruction, even when that destruction comes from within. Beloved, we must find our fire, protect it, and pass it on.

Original Poems and Poetics on Fire

> *"CATCH YOUR FIRE... DON'T KILL*
> *HOLD YOUR FIRE... DON'T KILL*
> *LEARN YOUR FIRE... DON'T KILL*
> *BE THE FIRE... DON'T KILL..."*
>
> AN EXCERPT FROM CATCH THE FIRE BY SONIA SANCHEZ, BLACK ARTS MOVEMENT POET, 1995.

In the immortal words of Sanchez, "Hold your fire! Don't kill!" Don't fight police fire with community fires. In conclusion, a dualistic trope of love and hate is central to our work. Yes, we must begin to measure the extremes of love and hate, like the fire of hatred and anti-black racism that works against the fire of the love of justice. We are called to fight fire with fire. That is, we are fighting the fire of hatred with the fire of love. And love is going to win the day! Where is your fire? We need more fire in the form of community activism and advocacy.

After the Fire

There's healing after the fire
Once hate has been burned down
There is room
Room for redemption
Fire of love consumes wild hatred
In the hearts of men
Hate that grows
Is watered by fear

Fire

Fire and Imagination

Internal heat of blood
Runs warm through veins
Sparks of flame
Sprinkle seeds of possibility
Rhythm of fire
Animates life within
Phallic flames consummate the dream
Birthing the universe
From hidden interior worlds
Always burning
Sets our minds ablaze
A veiled flame in the belly of the beast
Like a refining fire
Between Heaven and Earth
From an inferno
The potential of the heart burns

Fire and the Gaze

Fire watchers put eyes on me
Peepers putting me in my place
Hypnotic eyes tell lies
Staring hard to make me their slave
When will those eyes
Gaze upon a mirror?

Fire

Fire and Respect

Fire is a privileged phenomenon
It explains anything
Intimate and universal
Explains that which changes quickly
It is a living element in our hearts, in the sky
From the depths of substance to the warmth of love
Fire can retreat into substance and hide
It shines in heaven and burns in hell
It can be gentle and torture
It pleasures and punishes,
Is both good and bad
The first thing we learn is not to touch fire
Because fire devours
Above all, fire commands respect

Chapter Four

Conclusion
Breath / Voice / Fire: Justice Of The Heart

> "Somewhere there's gotta be,
> Somebody who can hear my deepest plea,
> Someday there's gotta be . . .
> Justice of the heart,
> Here just for me."[1]
>
> —Lyrics from "Justice of the Heart," Written by Stevie Wonder & Brenda Russell, 2002

Part I: A Letter to the Ancestor, George Floyd

For Those Who Have Gone On.
For Those Who Remain.

Inasmuch as a letter can be written to an otherworldly being absent from the material world, I write to you today, George Floyd, with so much on my mind and so much to say in my heart. I write to you today with a true sense of moral urgency to let you know

---

1. Wonder and Russell, "Justice of the Heart."

Conclusion

that we still need you and cling dearly to your memory for what your life and untimely demise represent. Also, I write to tell you that you are one of our ancestors now, and with this divine appointment in the celestial realm, there are a few things you should be made aware of.

First, please know that this coveted ancestral role you possess comes with specific duties and responsibilities. In case you did not know, ancestors are of the utmost critical importance to those of us who remain. Here. Lost. In someone else's homeland, we can never indeed lay our entire claim. Here we remain in an American wilderness without an accurate, trustworthy compass to guide us to a safe path for living in this complicated land. Here we remain, not knowing what to do about the age-old, cryptic riddle trapped inside an enigma: The *American race* problem.

Now more than ever, we need our trusted ancestors' wisdom—those who have shed innocent blood on this land for no justifiable reason. We need your guidance as this shortsighted, absent-minded country with everything to gain and nothing to lose must begin the tedious work of achieving racial equality. If America will move toward healing and get past its white supremacy legacy of hatred, of which your personal story is now a part, we will need your guidance. We need you now for those who remain as modern generations see a terrifying version of America. Millennials and Generations Y and Z somehow believed racism was either nonexistent or an ancient relic of the distant past, and are now living in shock, amazed to learn for the first time how racist America still is, today. We need to hold dear our communal memory of you. Like a feeling of déjà vu and the deep longing in the pit of our being that reassures our minds that we have been here before, we cling to the memory of how we watched your reluctant spirit transition from life to death.

We adhere to this memory because we do not know how not to and still go on. For those who remain, we need to hold dear the power of your voice as we continue to be haunted by the hallowedness of your final words. We journeyed with you as you transitioned from this strange land of America to the promised land of heavenly hosts. We need to hold dear your spirit and the passion of your fire that set the world ablaze and mobilized a global resistance movement like no other protest in modern American history.

America still has a long way to go to meet the dream of the idealized mountaintop conceived by hope and faith and delivered by love fifty-nine years ago by another martyr named Dr. King. Those who remain are still striving to get there with only the memory of our breath, voice, and fire to connect to our communal trauma. We still have the final frontier to explore and conquer, the heart. Anti-black racism still lives in the hearts of too many Americans. The struggle continues here in the land of the living, and there are new challenges to tackle as a shooter killed ten primarily black Americans at a supermarket in Buffalo, New York, last week. A senseless tragedy that causes us to question how much progress has been made since your death. But we are hopeful, and we seek your counsel. We continue to fight the good fight knowing that God is on the side of the righteous. It will not be long before we arrive at our true destiny. Strides are being made. Our souls cling to hope and love, so we will be granted the power to change hearts.

I find it of the utmost importance to say to you: your life mattered. Truly. Your life still matters, even in your death. In this, I mean that your life was significant, even if the tragic outcome was something you and your family did not foresee. And although you and so many other black bodies in police custody died much too soon in the most arrogant and offensive state-sanctioned ways, your short life, particularly its ending, taught us so much about man's inhumanity to man. Your death taught us the importance of seeing the heart of our fellow man. Thus, your public death exposed something profoundly profane about America to Americans. The year 2020 will forever be etched in the hearts of its daughters and sons and stepdaughters and stepsons alike. What was revealed and what America reluctantly learned from your death was that America has a severe heart problem related to justice and the lack

Conclusion

thereof, for all its greatness and exceptionalism. Does this country have a heart at all? It's much like the ictional character the Tin Man in *The Wizard of Oz*, who opens the chest cavity where the heart should reside and finds an empty, vacant vessel.

Is America's identity like the Tin Man, who cannot be who he is fully intended to be until he goes to the Wizard to procure a heart? Perhaps. Whether the heart must be obtained or if it is already there hidden beneath the surface, this matter is of no consequence. But one thing is sure: Once the heart *is* located, America must begin to take self-inventory and ask itself, "What is *in* this nation's heart?" Love or hatred? Courage or fear? Does America have a heart, or is it America heartless like the Tin Man? Your killing, George, grievous as it was, served as the ultimate mirror that showed America the wretched, uncompassionate condition of its heart. Your murder allowed the country to see its ugliness and hypocrisy through hard-hearted police policies like the one that allowed the legal application of a lethal choke hold.

George Floyd, we will never forget your last breath and how you called on your maternal ancestor, Cissy, in those final moments. We will never forget your last words taking form as a voice in your last minutes of life. You spoke to us as you transitioned home. And we will never forget the spark of your spirit setting the world on fire until it burst into the flames of righteous indignation. Your story was what fueled the fire of resistance during one of the most challenging times in modern American history. For the first time, the world noticed what could happen to black bodies in America while in police custody. Believe me, my brother, we will never forget your transforming breath, voice, and fire and how your singular story changed the world in many ways.

As an ancestor now, please know that we will never forget the transformative hope your death gave us, what George Floyd's narrative means to the American narrative, and how it will be read for generations to come. As unfortunate and untimely as it was, your death symbolized transition, transformation, and transcendence for this country on racial equality. It marked a change in how community policing will be conducted. America still has a long way to go. But for those of us from the resistance who remain, we need your guidance on how best to fix America's heart.

And for those who remain, we must not press on and not grieve for you too long. The demanding work of healing this divided nation is now upon us. Who will ensure America's future as a democratic, diverse, and inclusive nation? Black Americans who dare to believe in the philosophy of *Never Stop Breathing* are destined to carry this nation into the future. And for those who remain in the land of the living, our hearts take solace in knowing that people of all shades, creeds, and ethnicities stood together in solidarity with black Americans to mourn the atrocity of your blatant murder.

We were not the "others" on the days immediately following your demise. For a moment in time, we had the world's full attention. If only for one moment, the moral arc of the universe had temporarily bent toward justice, as witnessed by a divided society's unanimous response of outrage. People united with black Americans, and the resistance chanted "I can't breathe" as citizens of America would soon learn that others from the African Diaspora had experienced *exactly* what you experienced: A tragic, unexplained, unjustifiable death while being detained by police and held in custody. These other victims even pleaded for their lives in the same manner to no avail. These countless souls also informed the officers that they could not breathe, just as you did, and lost their lives the same way you did.

On that day, we were all George Floyd. You died so mercilessly that we all knew what happened to you could happen to any black American. Those who remain can be subjected to the harsh realities of racial profiling because of the toxic white supremacy ideologies that believe we do not "belong" in America. For those of us who remain, we ask you, one among our dearly departed ancestors, to show us the best path to navigate through the heart of humanity in ways that institute substantive change on the issue of racial justice and equity in this country. For those of us who

Conclusion

remain, we do so wholeheartedly as we know that the ancestors, including you now, have been charged with guiding our steps and shining a light on the dark places in America's heart that are causing this nation to disintegrate before our eyes.

One last thing. It's about Derek Chauvin. The Minneapolis police officer fatally lodged his knee on your neck for eight minutes and forty-six seconds. I must speak about him as we still have so many unanswered questions about his motivation to take your life in such a deliberate manner. What was in his heart on that day? One must ascertain that hatred was in his heart as he choked the last breath out of your body. Naked, unabashed hatred. The kind that takes a lifetime to mature and perfect; one that cultivates itself carefully and meticulously into a full-blown rage grown up enough to harbor the callousness and cruelty needed to publicly end a man's life with no fear of consequences or repercussions.

The murderous act was memorialized on phone video and uploaded on the internet for the world to see. One would have to conclude that hatred in his heart caused him not to hear the desperate plea for mercy in your heart. What kind of hatred is this that Chauvin possesses? It's that kind of hatred hidden so deep that it introduces a man to himself. And then, finally, he forever knows what kind of monster he is and of what he is capable. One could ask, "What was the voice in Chauvin's heart saying to him in those last moments of publicly taking a man's life?" Was that voice telling him, "Enough already! Let this man live." Or was the voice saying, "He has suffered enough. Let this man breathe before he chokes to death!" What was the voice in Chauvin's heart saying about Floyd's breath? Eliminate it? Perhaps. Bob Marley penned the lyric, "Kill them before they grow."

We will never know the answers to these intimate details about what was in Chauvin's heart on that day. But it was evident that the passion of hatred for black bodies burned in the heart of this officer. From this fire of hate, the voice in Chauvin's heart led him to

Breath | Voice | Fire

eliminate your breath on that day. With no remorse, in the most self-righteous, indignant manner, bearing a sinister smirk and a psychotic smile on his face, your life was stolen. From the fire to the voices to the breath, the connection is clear: what we find in a man's heart has the power to control his actions positively or negatively. So, we must guard our hearts ferociously so that we might protect our breath, voice, and fire as a means of pure survival.

George Floyd, what you had in your heart was a passionate love of your life and a fierce desire to protect your breath from the system of white supremacy that claimed you for its own sake. We thanked God for the video footage collected by a bystander and made public on the internet, or we would never have known the full extent of what happened to you at the crime scene. Had it not been for the video, we would never have known how clearly and precisely you raised your voice in defense of your life to let Chauvin understand that you could not breathe and that you were going to die. We all witnessed you tell Officer Chauvin repeatedly that your neck and throat could no longer sustain the weight of his body. We all heard your voice, clear and compelling; it just was not enough to melt the hard heart of this rogue officer. Once you transitioned and your earthly life was no more, the embodiment of your life, including your tragic demise, became the spark that fueled resistance protests worldwide. Millions of people chanted your name. But to what end?

Is there "justice of the heart" for you, George Floyd? Is there someone who would hear your simple plea for life? Not on that day, May 25, 2020. From this simple lyric penned by two of my favorite songwriters, I submit that there was not a justice of the heart for you. The cries you offered. You repeatedly uttered the deepest plea through faded half breaths, "I can't breathe. I can't breathe." When we listen to you with our hearts, we hear you saying to Chauvin, "Let the punishment fit the crime." Never in the history of America has the passing of a counterfeit bill, inadvertently or deliberately, been considered a violent crime punishable by death. Yet, American police department statutes permit officers to use a controversial choke hold with fatal ramifications in the "pursuit of justice."

Conclusion

Chauvin failed to see the man's humanity fighting for survival beneath his knee in his pursuit of justice. He was disconnected. Chauvin was disconnected from himself, his fellow man, and God. He did not connect to the heart and soul of the man he was so casually resting upon with all proof of privilege and power. For all of Chauvin's hubris, another justice should have prevailed that day. That is the justice that does not penalize mercilessly but hears the plea of a dying man's heart and responds in kind with love and compassion. None of us can accurately attest to knowing precisely what is in the heart of someone. That notion is an impossibility. But we can learn something about a man's heart based on his actions.

Justice never found its way to Chauvin's heart. After being found guilty on three counts, including second-degree unintentional murder, second-degree manslaughter, and third-degree murder, he entered a plea agreement and was sentenced to twenty-two years. Much has happened to Chauvin since his original sentencing. But one thing is sure: his heart remains the same. In April 2022, we learned that Chauvin is seeking an appeal for the sentence he now serves for killing you. I fear what will happen in America if his conviction is somehow overturned due to the rocky political climate we find ourselves in. We now and forever reside in a world where the legacy of George Floyd has, in the words of your daughter, Gianna, "changed the world."

For those of us who remain, we do so with the hope for better community relations with the law enforcement officers charged with the duty of protecting the community, not killing it slowly, and with no regard for the humanity of the black citizens in this country. Because of your legacy, police departments are getting their houses in order swiftly, and innovative approaches to community policing are being implemented. But the police departments alone are not the problem. White supremacy in America is. And for that, unfortunately, there is no easy remedy. Because of the significance of your death in American history, those who remain do so with hope and courage in their hearts because we now know what one life can do to bring about change. For those who remain in this strange land known as America, we need not be brokenhearted or give up on hope for the future.

In your example, we learned much. If we protect our breath, raise our voices, and remain on fire for justice, one singular life can spark the flame that brings about that kind of resistance that can change the world. Just like you, George Floyd. Our beloved, watchful ancestor. In your name and for your sacrifice, the struggle continues. *We will never stop breathing!*

Eternally,

The Psalmist

Part II. Justice of The Heart

1. Introduction: What's in Your Heart?

How does one respond to racial injustice without examining what is in one's heart? What does the heart know intuitively about the topic of justice? What can the heart teach us about the depth of human compassion required for systemic change as we strive to achieve racial equality in America? The guiding principle that responds to the enigma of race remains: What's in your heart? Love or hate? Courage or fear? We can all agree that the answers to many of life's most profound mysteries often reside in the heart. The heart, more than anything, has a dualism within its very nature that divides what we know and what we understand by differentiating between what we love and hate.

Regardless of the nature of the subject, all matters are decided by what is in the heart of a person, how we love or hate our sisters and brothers. Which lives are deemed worthy, and which lives are expendable? These moral and ethical judgments are all matters of the heart to be decided based on love, hate, courage, or fear. Dare I say that if love prevails in one's heart, one's actions will be deemed more just than if hate is the predominant emotion.

Justice characterizes God's wisdom. All aspects of the human—the mind, body, soul, spirit, and heart—are subject to

Conclusion

rebuke for the rejection of God's wisdom, as the rejection of God's wisdom is the rejection of justice. We find this true through many examples and relevant instances through biblical analysis. Hebrews 4:12–13 reads, "Indeed, the word of God is living and active and sharper than any two-edged sword, piercing until it divides soul from spirit, joints from marrow; it can judge the thoughts and intentions of the heart. And before him, no creature is hidden, but all are naked and laid bare to the eyes of the one to whom we must render an account." Thus, it is our thoughts and intentions that we cannot hide from rebuke. Our thoughts and actions can be judged as rejecting justice or godly wisdom.

As we grapple with knowing our truth and the objective truth about our world, we find that our humanness hinders us from fully understanding the truth about justice. Thus, it is difficult for us to fully know the concept of justice as she is often hidden in plain sight. Justice is hidden in the heart and can only be found by those who dare to search deep enough into the heart and mental consciousness to find her. Ideally, this is the way we should understand justice. But justice simply means different things to different people. The term *justice* has many faces and is often constructed to justify a particular outcome. Justice is also understood through the heart as the physical embodiment of our lived experiences. Juxtaposed against the backdrop of an unjust world, justice, that elusive construct that constantly mocks us, is daring us to find her. To catch her if we can!

Hosea 12:6 says, "Hold fast to love and justice." This is easier said than done because both are hard to catch and hold. But when these two entities, love and justice, are indeed possessed in the heart, there is hope for this lost world. When love and justice abide, there also can truth abide. And when the truth abides, then we are not afraid. We can trust it. We can believe in the world we created and that our world can achieve a greater degree of equity and equality for all citizens.

Yet there is still the issue of the dualistic nature of the heart and what one finds in the dark places of the heart, like white supremacy that leads to anti-black violence. Jeremiah 17:9 reads,

"The heart is deceitful above all things and beyond cure. Who can understand it?" For example, take a generally good person, like a neighbor you know, who secretly harbors bigoted feelings toward others. Thus, every person must know the darkest regions of their heart so that they do not find themselves perpetrating acts of hatred against their fellow brothers and sisters. The heart also has a precise mechanism of intuitive knowledge known as the wisdom of the heart.

Psalm 90:12:17 states, "So teach us to number our days, that we may gain a heart of wisdom." A heart of wisdom rightly assesses that which is just. That is, wisdom as it relates to a more equitable worldview. But the hard hearts of people (both the officers and citizens) who rejected God's justice in the face of protest on behalf of George Floyd and other victims of racial hatred must expect a rebuke for their heartless actions. What is in their hearts? For this answer, one must consider a deeper look at the relationship between one's heart and actions.

2. Heart and Stone

"A new heart I will give you, and a new spirit I will put within you, and I will remove from your body the heart of stone and give you a heart of flesh."

—Ezekiel 36:26

The human heart can be understood as a cosmic vessel that shapes our moral consciousness and directs our actions in the world. Proverbs 4:23 states, "Above all else, guard your heart, for everything you do flows from it." Thus, in its emotional state, the heart governs the mind's decision-making process and the body's actions. How humanity conducts itself in a given society directly reflects the condition of the hearts of human beings that comprise that society. From the beating hearts of the people on earth, we create our communities—good or bad. It all begins with what is in

Conclusion

the heart. The question is whether American society has been built from hearts of stone or hearts of flesh.

One can determine the condition of the people's hearts by assessing the policies, laws, and community rules that govern and organize the civic life of individuals. Are the American lawmakers governing with hearts of stone? This can be assessed by the way they administer justice. Again, the question is: What's in their hearts? Love or hatred? Courage or fear? Are these individuals prepared to receive condemnation for their unjust laws and the heartless way they are administered? Isaiah 10 says, "Woe to those who make unjust laws, to those who issue oppressive decrees to deprive the poor of their rights and withhold justice from the oppressed of my people, making widows their prey and robbing the fatherless. What will you do on the day of reckoning when disaster comes from afar?"

Take the individuals who created the justice system that governs America. In their case, there may be a day of reckoning in their future for one reason and one reason only: They are ruling over the people without first examining the condition of their hearts to discern whether their statutes are in line with the principles of love and justice or hatred and evil. The rebuke may be inevitable for America. No one knows what will happen in the end. A rebuke of America may be needed to get America to where societal change can come about. Jeremiah 17:10 states, "I the Lord test the mind and search the heart, to give to all according to their ways, according to the fruit of their doings."

As the people suffer in this nation from the effects of anti-black racism in all its forms, those in power who have not responded earnestly to the cries of black Americans like George Floyd, there may come a time when they will need to answer for the mistreatment of black citizens. There is a sense of self-awareness required for each policymaker at the state, local, and federal levels to understand the mind-heart connection and how the emotional disposition of the heart impacts one's moral consciousness as policy decisions are made. A hard heart of hatred will always yield hard-hearted policies that hurt the communities they are charged with helping.

Thus, the lawmakers who have worked to create an unjust society built on white supremacy will be judged. Unrighteous lawmakers will not be able to hide from their hearts. What would be the way to assess the justice of the heart for these unjust lawmakers? The answer may reside in the response from Ezekiel: "A new heart I will give you, and a new spirit I will put within you, and I will remove from your body the heart of stone and give you a heart of flesh." As a woman of faith, I believe that as America goes through this transition, hearts of stone will be transformed into hearts of flesh and that love will transcend hate.

3. A Call for Action: Where Is Your Breath, Voice, Fire?

In the spirit of Sonia Sanchez, I say, "Where is your breath?" "Where is your voice?" "Where is your fire?" The first step needed for racial justice is the challenging task of locating one's breath, finding one's voice, discovering one's fire, and understanding the relationship between these three elements. One could imagine the three aspects of the breath, voice, and fire trope as a manifestation of justice understood through the heart. How does this trope work together through the heart, and why does it matter in the work of social activism? Collectively, breath, voice, and fire all reside in the heart. These elements represent the survival of the human spirit as it endures societal injustice. It connects to the heart to understand how justice works, as the beating heart is fundamental to human existence.

All three elements combined produce the heartbeat that defines the rhythm that is the song of life. Most importantly, the breath, voice, and fire trope describes the unspoken passion for justice that we all feel but may not always be able to express fully. Thus, all three elements must express an intense love for justice. It can also be understood as a survival trope by highlighting the importance of preserving breath, raising our voices, and stoking our fire. Collectively, breath, voice, and fire all work from the heart in ways that lead to justice.

One does not have to look further than one's own heart to unlock the relational importance of this breath, voice, and fire in

Conclusion

addressing racial justice. In all its mysterious ways, the heart helps us understand why this trope matters for the discourse on social justice. Since all three elements are connected to the heart, we can illuminate various aspects of the fight for racial justice by viewing it through multiple lenses. Individually, the breath relates to the heart by bringing oxygen to the chamber of the vessel. Voice connects to the heart through the consciousness of the mind. Fire connects to the heart as the intuitive interpretation of our passions and desires. We have the road map to respond to the *"Never Stop Breathing"* mandate with the command of our individual and collective breath, voice, and fire.

Chapter Five

Epilogue
Never Stop Breathing

Breath | Voice | Fire as Faith in Action

Years have passed since George Floyd's murder, and we have more questions than answers. How much progress on police reform has been made since the protests of 2020? Does the average American citizen know what it means to be anti-racist? What solutions have been implemented to address the roots of white supremacy at the systemic level in the American political, economic, and social contexts?

One could assess that on the issues of racial equality, America is and will always be a work in progress. However, this nation's unresolved race issues have proven to be detrimental to the country's public health, as unresolved racism often leads to violent outcomes. Therefore, I ask the question: Have we as a nation witnessed any progress in this country on the issue of race? As the police killings post-Floyd continue, we must now pause to unpack the mass shootings and the attacks on innocent black people based on extremist notions of a "Great Replacement Theory." Now more than ever before, America would do well to begin to look at the heart of our nation and determine whether or not it is truly a democratic nation inclusive of everyone. As an homage to George

Epilogue

Floyd's death, one thing we can learn is the importance of the mandate to *Never Stop Breathing!*

For the entire time I was in graduate school at Drew University, from 2015 to 2022, America was going through an existential crisis. At the core of its struggle is the struggle for identity. This identity problem found itself center stage at the onset of the presidential campaign of Donald J. Trump, where the candidate stoked the fires of racism and xenophobia from day one until he was ushered out in an insurrectionist blaze of violence, dishonor, and disgrace. Then he was elected in 2024 for a second term. Which America are you a part of? Trump's America or the Resistance's America? I must say those were, and still are, interesting times. A lot of sleepless nights for the Resistance. But we were united in our disdain for a candidate who changed the American landscape in frightening ways.

We had the Black Lives Matter movement rise into the collective consciousness of the world for the first time since its inception in 2013. By the time we witnessed the murder of George Floyd, the Resistance was well organized and ready to respond to the issue of racial profiling and people dying in police custody. As a graduate student, I felt helpless while all this was going on. But because I am a writer, I wrote. I developed this trope of Breath | Voice | Fire to express the moment's intensity based on what our world felt like during this remarkable period in American history. From one black American woman's point of view, I wrote poetry, prose, and protest songs and spoke up. I wrote for a little-known literary genre classified as social justice writing. And yes, it felt great.

In 2019, while in graduate school, under the direction of Dr. Kenneth Ngwa, I began to get involved with the Bible and culture division's new research area in religion and health. My initial interest in working with religion and health involved ways to bring music, spirituality, and healing into the religion, health, and science discourse. I was one of only two graduate students who presented my work at Harvard Medical School that year as part of the religion panel hosted by the Forum. By the following year, 2020, Dr. Ngwa had launched his concept into a fully supported partnership between Harvard Medical School and Drew Theological School, known as the Religion and Global Health Forum, to which I was blessed to instantly secure a spot as a doctoral research associate. Through this partnership, I received additional clinical research training at Brigham and Women's Hospital at Harvard Medical School. I now serve as affiliated faculty for the Forum's Doctor of Ministry program in Faith, Health, and Social Equity.

My life has not been the same since I joined this research project. We worked diligently to set up the administrative infrastructure for the Forum before the opening event, which was a public launch of the initiative held at Drew in February 2020. As soon as we settled into our tasks for the day-to-day operations, we were notified by the school's administration that the campus would be shut down for everyone's safety in response to the COVID-19 pandemic. As instructed, the professor and the two research students closed our offices and retreated to our respective homes, where we would continue our work via Zoom. We responded to COVID-19 with educational programming and advocacy around the new virus that would now rule all our lives. We continued producing virtual events and meeting with new partners to alleviate community fears about COVID and health disparities based on race. We also worked to equip the community churches with the information and resources needed to serve stigmatized neighborhoods on the front lines.

Then, George Floyd's tragic killing on May 25, 2020, was made public via a bystander video. Again, my life was never the same. Seeing Floyd die on video can be likened to how my mother and father must have felt when they saw newspaper images of Emmett Till's unrecognizable body in the open casket during his public funeral. The Religion and Global Health team was devastated by this national travesty of Floyd's death. Dr. Ngwa shifted focus for the rest of the summer to respond to the overwhelming outpouring of community grief and loss that we all experienced, compounded by fear of the pandemic, which disproportionately impacted black Americans. That August, after three months of a global protest over George Floyd, police violence, and racial profiling, Dr. Ngwa

Epilogue

responded with the launch of the Never Stop Breathing initiative. The impetus for the Religion and Health Forum taking this initiative under its umbrella was because, following the lead of the American Medical Association's reporting, "Racism had now been declared a public health threat in America."

This new community of artists, activists, and scholars perfectly suited me. It gave me an authentic space to imagine and envision my epistemology related to my Breath | Voice | Fire research. I developed the curriculum, gave classroom lectures on my research under the Religion and Global Health Forum's Never Stop Breathing platform, and learned firsthand what modern students felt about what was happening to our world during these uncertain times.

Following the resistance activism related to the dual pandemics of anti-black racism and COVID-19 kept me remarkably busy with educational writing and curriculum as a doctoral researcher and clinical research trainee. Each day was an adventure as I tried to imagine, moment by moment, what Breath | Voice | Fire could mean for this current moment. Our hearts were on a roller coaster as we moved with the nation to respond to the day's crises. More than anything, I wanted people who engaged with my writing and curriculum to glean spiritual healing through the mechanisms of transition, transformation, and transcendence. Through Breath | Voice | Fire, I wanted people to feel a sense of hope and progress on racial justice through the understanding of justice moving us through transition, transformation, and transcendence.

All the educational and advocacy programs we produced informed my artistic interpretation and helped me to fully understand the potentiality of the Breath | Voice | Fire trope as the cornerstone for my future advocacy work. In the chaos of one moment in time, this beautiful expression of the heart (Breath | Voice | Fire) became the source from which my work flowed, one that I am proud to produce today with the guidance of the ancestors who live among us even today.

My time with the Religion and Global Health Forum and the Never Stop Breathing initiative has given me the foundation for understanding how we imagine justice in a creative, transformative, transcendent manner. Dr. Ngwa's teaching on the mandate "Why We Won't Stop Breathing" has given this Breath | Voice | Fire trope new life today and a new perspective. For as long as we have our breath, as long as we have our voice, and for as long as we have our fire, we will never stop breathing. No pandemics of coronavirus or racial violence will cause us to succumb. We have everything needed to survive any virus that comes our way. Whether it be the virus of the body or the virus of racism, this newly adapted worldview of Never Stop Breathing, as created by Dr. Ngwa and inspired by George Floyd, will guide us as we transcend hatred with love, saying it as often as needed, Black Lives Matter. #BlackBreathMatters, #BlackVoiceMatters, #BlackFireMatters.

Bibliography

Baldwin, Hannah. "bell hooks and the growth of intersectionality in Western feminism." *Manchester Historian*, April 22, 2020. manchesterhistorian.com/2020/bell-hooks-and-the-growth-of-intersectionality-in-western-feminism-by-hannah-baldwin/.

Baldwin, James. "The American Dream and the American Negro." *The New York Times*, March 7, 1965. https://archive.nytimes.com/www.nytimes.com/books/98/03/29/specials/baldwin-dream.html?_r=1&oref=login.

———. "Baldwin-Buckley Cambridge University Debate of 1965." https://www.rimaregas.com/2015/06/transcript-james-baldwin-debates-william-f-buckley-1965-blog42/.

———. *Collected Essays*. Ann Arbor: University of Michigan Press, 1998.

———. *I Am Not Your Negro*. (A Film by Raoul Peck.) New York: Vintage, 2016.

———. "My Dungeon Shook/A Letter for My Nephew." In *The Fire Next Time*, 1–10. New York: Vintage International, 1993.

Bellot, Gabrielle. "The Famous Baldwin-Buckley Debate Still Matters Today." *The Atlantic*, December 2, 2019. https://www.theatlantic.com/entertainment/archive/2019/12/james-baldwin/william-f-buckley-debate/602695/.

Bridgeman, Valerie. "A Long Way from Home: Displacement, Lament, and Singing Protest in Psalm 137." *Perspectives in Religious Studies* 44 (2016) 213-23.

Camus, Albert. *The Myth of Sisyphus*. New York: Random House, 2018.

———. *The Plague*. New York: Vintage International, 1948.

———. *The Rebel: An Essay on Man in Revolt*. New York: Vintage International, 1956.

Carroll, Charles. *The Negro: A Beast or in the Image of God*. St. Louis: American Book and Bible House, 1900.

Carter, Ryan. "LA Riots 30 Years Later: From 'City on Fire' to the George Floyd Era." *Los Angeles Daily News*, April 29, 2022.

Bibliography

CBS Mornings. "Note to Self: Congressman John Lewis on the 'Moral Obligation' to 'Speak Up.'" June 29, 2017. https://www.cbsnews.com/news/note-to-self-congressman-john-lewis-civil-rights-leader/.

Coles, Robert. "James Baldwin Back Home." *The New York Times,* July 31, 1977.

Diagne, Souleymane Bachir. "Négritude." *The Stanford Encyclopedia of Philosophy* (Summer 2018 ed.), edited by Edward N. Zalta. https://plato.stanford.edu/archives/sum2018/entries/negritude/.

Dimock, Michael, and Richard Wike. "America Is Exceptional in the Nature of Its Political Divide." Pew Research Center, November 13, 2020. https://www.pewresearch.org/short-reads/2020/11/13/america-is-exceptional-in-the-nature-of-its-political-divide/.

Dominican Sisters of Peace Missions. https://oppeace.org/.

Dominican Sisters of Peace. "Preach the Truth in a Million Voices." April 30, 2019. https://springfieldop.org/wp-content-uploads/JTM-2017-September.pdf.

Dostoevsky, Fyodor. *The Brothers Karamazov.* New York: Bantam Dell, 2003.

———. *Crime and Punishment.* New York: Liveright, 2018.

———. *The Idiot.* London: Penguin, 2004.

Du Bois, W. E. B. *The Souls of Black Folk.* New York: Dover, 1994.

Fanon, Frantz. *Black Skin, White Masks.* Rev. ed. New York: Grove, 2008.

———. *A Dying Colonialism,* New York: Grove, 1994.

Falkner, William. *Requiem for a Nun.* New York: Vintage International, 2011.

Gale, William G., and Darrell M. West. "Is the US Headed for Another Civil War?" The Brookings Institute, September 16, 2021. https://www.brookings.edu/articles/is-the-us-headed-for-another-civil-war/.

Gordon, Lewis R. *An Introduction to Africana Philosophy.* Cambridge: Cambridge University Press, 2009.

Hahn, Thich Nhat. *The Miracle of Mindfulness: An Introduction to the Practice of Meditation.* Boston: Beacon, 2016.

hooks, bell. *All About Love: New Visions.* New York: William Morrow, 2018.

———. *Feminist Theory: From Margins to Center.* New York: Routledge Taylor Francis Group, 2015.

———. *Remembering Rapture: The Writer at Work.* New York: St. Martin's, 1999.

Holmes, Barbara A. *Crisis Contemplation: Healing the Wounded Village.* Albuquerque, NM: Center for Action and Contemplation, 2021.

Hughes, Langston. "I, Too." In *The Collected Poems of Langston Hughes,* 46. New York: Knopf and Vintage, 1994.

Jones, Martha. "America Was Forged by the Marginalized." *The New York Times,* October 22, 2021.

Kennedy, John Fitzgerald. "Address to Canadian Parliament in 1961." https://millercenter.org/the-presidency/presidential-speeches/may-17-1961-address-canadian-parliament.

King, Martin Luther, Jr. "Letter from a Birmingham Jail." Atlanta: Martin Luther King Jr. Center for Nonviolent Social Change, 1968.

Bibliography

———. "Remaining Awake Through a Great Revolution." Speech at the National Cathedral, March 31, 1968. https://www.newamericanjournal.net/2023/02/martin-luther-kings-final-speech-on-remaining-awake-through-a-great-revolution/.

Lincoln, Abraham. "Emancipation Proclamation." January 1, 1863. https://millercenter.org/the-presidency/presidential-speeches-january-1-1863-the-emancipation-proclamation.

———. "The House Divided." June 6, 1858. https://millercenter.org/the-presidency/presidential-speeches/june-16-1858-house-divided-speech.

Morgan, Anthony. "Black Life and the Myth of Sisyphus." *St. Louis American*. https://www.stlamerican.com/news/editorials/black-america-and-the-myth-of-sisyphus/.

Morin, Rebecca. "John Lewis: 'Some forces in America trying to take us back to another period.'" *Politico*, September 18, 2016. https://www.politico.com/story/2016/09/john-lewis-some-forces-in-america-trying-to-take-us-back-to-another-period-228333.

Morrison, Toni. "An Interview With Toni Morrison and Charlie Rose." Charlie Rose, May 7, 1993. https://charlierose.com/videos/18778.

———. *Beloved*. London: Everyman, 2006.

———. "No Place for Self-Pity, No Room for Fear." *The Nation*, March 23, 2015. https://www.thenation.com/article/archive/no-place-for-self-pity-no-room-fear/.

Ng, Celeste. *Little Fires Everywhere*. New York: Penguin, 2017.

"Nobody Knows the Trouble I See." Negro spiritual.

"Over My Head." *The Spirituals Database*. http://spirituals-database.com/omeka/items/show/6434.

Porter, Dawn, dir. *John Lewis: Good Trouble*. New York: Magnolia Pictures, 2020.

Prewitt, Kenneth. "Why the Announcement of a Looming White Minority Makes Demographers Nervous." *The New York Times*, November 22, 2008.

Ruiz-Grossman, Sarah. "At Least 2,000 More Black Americans Were Lynched Than Previously Reported." *HuffPost*, June 17, 2020. huffpost.com/entry/lynchings-black-americans-reconstruction-eji-report-n_5eea6f94c5b6d4397ade568a.

Sadler, Rodney S., Jr. "Genesis." In *The Africana Bible: Reading Israel's Scriptures from Africa and the African Diaspora*, edited by Hugh R. Page Jr., 70–79. Minneapolis: Fortress, 2010.

Sanchez, Sonia. "Catch the Fire." In *Wounded in the House of a Friend*. Boston: Beacon, 1995.

Santayana, George. *The Life of Reason: Critical Edition*. Cambridge: MIT Press, 2011.

Shange, Ntozake. *For Colored Girls Who Have Considered Suicide/When the Rainbow Is Enuf: A Choreopoem*. Rev. ed. New York: Scribner, 2010.

Simone, Nina. "An Artist's Duty." https://www.youtube.com/watch?v=99VomMNf5fo.

Bibliography

Škof, Lenart. *Breath of Proximity: Intersubjectivity, Ethics, and Peace*. London: Springer, 2015.

Smith, James K. A. *Thinking in Tongues: Pentecostal Contributions to Christian Philosophy*. Grand Rapids: Eerdmans, 2010.

Wallis, Jim. *America's Original Sin: Racism, White Privilege, and the Bridge to a New America*. Grand Rapids: Brazos, 2016.

West, Cornel. *Black Prophetic Fire*. Boston: Beacon, 2014.

West, Cornel. *Brother West: Living and Loving Out Loud, a Memoir*. 2nd ed. New York: Smiley, 2010.

Wonder, Stevie, and Brenda Russell. "Justice of the Heart." Track 5 on the to the *John Q*. Soundtrack, 2002. https://ringostrack.com/en/movie/john-q/26942.

www.ingramcontent.com/pod-product-compliance
Lightning Source LLC
Chambersburg PA
CBHW031459160426
43195CB00010BB/1025